VOLUME THREE

ALIGNING
WITH THE
APOSTOLIC

AN ANTHOLOGY OF APOSTLESHIP

APOSTLES AND APOSTOLIC MOVEMENT
IN THE SEVEN MOUNTAINS OF CULTURE

DR. BRUCE COOK
GENERAL EDITOR

Cover Design: Wendy K. Walters with James L. Nesbit

Interior Formatting: Wendy K. Walters

Published By KINGDOM HOUSE PUBLISHING | LAKEBAY, WASHINGTON, USA

To contact the Publisher or General Editor, call 253-858-8929 or text 512-845-3070, or email kingdomhousepublishing@gmail.com, or Skype: wbcook1, or visit:

www.KingdomHouse.net | www.KEYSnetwork.org
www.GloryRealm.net | www.VentureAdvisers.com

DEDICATION

TO THE CHIEF APOSTLE: JESUS, THE ONLY-BEGOTTEN SON OF GOD

(John 3:16-18, John 14:6, Rom. 8:32,
Rom. 10:9-13, 1 John 4:9-15)

*"Therefore, holy brothers, who share in the heavenly calling,
fix your thoughts on Jesus, the apostle and high
priest whom we confess."*
(Heb. 3:1, NIV)

AND TO THE NEXT GENERATION OF APOSTLES –

We Invite You to Stand Upon Our Shoulders

CONTRIBUTING AUTHORS

In Alphabetical Order

LaRue Adkinson

John Anderson, M.B.A.

David Andrade, Ph.D.

Doug Atha, D.S.L.

Ted Baehr, J.D., Hh.D.

Gary Beaton, B.A.

Ken Beaudry

Sharon Billins, B.S., Hh.D.

Laurie Boyd

Gordon Bradshaw, Ph.D., D.D.

Kari Browning

John Burpee, D.Min.

Philip Byler, D.R.E.

Duncan Campbell

Al Caperna, B.S.B.A.

Nick Castellano, Ph.D.

Bob Cathers, Hh.D.

Bruce Cook, Ph.D., Th.D.

Paul Cuny, B.A.

Tony Dale, M.D.

Stan DeKoven, Ph.D., D.Min.

Henry Falany

Tommi Femrite, D.P.M.

Charlie Fisher

Daniel Geraci

Berin Gilfillan, D.Min.

A.L. ("Papa") Gill, Ph.D.

Curtis Gillespie, B.S.B.A.

Max Greiner Jr., B.E.D.

Jon Grieser

Fernando Guillen, M.B.A.

Tim Hamon, Ph.D.

Mark Henderson

Robert Henderson, Hh.D.

Ray Hughes, D.D.

Kent Humphreys, B.A.

Christopher James

Stan Jeffery, M.B.A., D.Tech.

Bill Johnson, Hh.D.

Wende Jones, B.S.B.A.

Rick Joyner, Th.D.

Mark Kauffman, Ph.D.

Stephanie Klinzing

Erik Kudlis, Ph.D.

Candace Long, M.B.A.

Lee Ann Marino, Ph.D., D.D.

Joseph Mattera, D.Min.

Michelle Morrison, J.D.

CONTRIBUTING AUTHORS CONTINUED

John Muratori, D.C.L.

James Nesbit

Alice Patterson

Mark Pfeifer, B.A.

Lloyd Phillips, B.A.

Cal Pierce, B.S.B.A.

Walt Pilcher, M.B.A.

Paula Price, D.Min., Ph.D.

Gayle Rogers, Ph.D.

Morris Ruddick, B.S., M.S.

Michael Scantlebury, D.D.

Axel Sippach, Hh.D.

Kluane Spake, D.Min.

Tim Taylor, B.S.B.A.

Lorne Tebbutt

Ed Turose, B.S.B.A.

Larry Tyler, M.B.A.

Joseph Umidi, D.Min.

Thomas Webb, B.A., B.Th.

Arleen Westerhof, Ph.D.

Dick Westerhof, M.Eng.

Carl White Jr., D.D.

Dennis Wiedrick, B.A.

In addition to the General Editor, this multi-volume anthology was contributed to by 70 authors—almost all apostles and a few apostolic leaders; these are 70 spiritual elders in the body of Christ. Their contribution adds a depth of experience and authority to this historic work.

ADDITIONAL
MATERIALS

VOLUME THREE
ALIGNING WITH THE APOSTOLIC:
AN ANTHOLOGY OF APOSTLESHIP

This five-volume anthology represents an extensive body of work covering a wide range of topics discussing apostles and the apostolic. In order to keep the length of the volumes manageable, the General Editor has chosen to keep certain elements exclusive to Volume One. Each of these elements are an important part of the anthology as a whole, and reading them will provide you with a richer experience. We invite you to reference these materials in Volume One.

AVAILABLE IN VOLUME ONE:

"The Church, while an intrinsic part of the kingdom, is not the entirety of the kingdom. God's kingdom far outdistances the organizational, religious, and influential presence of the Church. It extends into every realm of culture, every corner of society, and every segment of ethnic identity. It is pervasive, manifesting its power and presence within the hearts and lives of those who have embraced Jesus Christ as Lord and King (Luke 17:21)."

Dr. Bruce Cook
General Editor of *Aligning With the Apostolic, An Anthology of Apostleship*

CONTENTS

SECTION V—APOSTOLIC CHARACTER & MATURITY

SECTION VI—APOSTOLIC EDUCATION

FOREWORD BY
DR. GORDON BRADSHAW

There are many mysteries surrounding the kingdom of God and as we advance into God's plans, the mysteries are gradually solved by way of revelation knowledge. One such mystery is the office of the apostle and the apostolic function as we have come to recognize and know it. Why the Lord Jesus Christ chose 12 men to become apostles and to usher the world into a new dimension is becoming more clear as God reveals His plan for apostles and apostolic influence today. We are the living extensions of the first apostolic display that Christ and the 12 apostles walked in but God is evolving that display to reach cultures, climates, customs and corporations beyond the basic scope of the religious community. It's bigger than many first believed.

Being a strong advocate of change, progress and advancement, I'm particularly fond of one of the best ways to educate humankind and how to share the fresh revelations that God gives to us. That method is called "revelation by writing and reading."

The apostle Paul stated, *"How that by revelation he made known unto me the mystery; (as I wrote afore in few words, Whereby when ye read ye may understand my knowledge in the mystery of Christ.) Which in other ages was not made known unto the sons of men as it is now revealed unto his holy apostles and prophets by the Spirit"* (Eph. 3:3-5, KJV). The days of strong revelation are here and apostles are an undeniable and important part of the revelation process. That process is stretching into every area of human activity and existence on the planet.

Eph. 3:3-5 strongly implies that there is more to come in the stream of revelation knowledge and dissolving of mysteries and that much of our expectation of things to come will be stimulated by reading. Books are an important part of the apostolic technology of revelation as described by the prophet Habakkuk. *"Write the vision, and make it plain upon tables, that he may run that readeth it"* (Hab. 2:2, KJV). Amazingly the word *'readeth'* translates from the Hebrew term *'Qara,'* meaning: To encounter, to publish and to address. Once people have read and understood the truth, they are able to *"run"* (*"Ruwts"*) or as the Hebrews translate it, they are able to break down, rush forward, divide speedily, run through things and reach their post. In other words, they are able to more quickly and efficiently reach their goals and fulfill their God-given destinies and purposes. I am grateful that Dr. Bruce Cook has captured the spirit of those revelations and has packaged the powerful revelations and experiences of so many apostles and apostolic people into this project.

This work by Dr. Bruce Cook, an apostle of apostles, is an incredible "Apostolic Masterpiece" destined to help individuals, families, ministries, businesses, corporations, governments and even nations apply apostolic principles. The fearless and unselfish task of inviting other apostolic agents to contribute to this writing further sharpened the "edge" of this book, making it one of, if not **the** most relevant book on apostolic "application technology" in our time. It 'decodes' many of the remaining 'mysteries' about apostolic assignments outside of the ministerial sphere and helps to describe the many diverse ways in which apostles and apostolic influences affect the world we live in. It also speaks to the tremendous "bridge building" abilities resident within Dr. Cook, making his work as a convener and advocate of all things apostolic, so important to us all. No longer will the apostleship be relegated to religious circles but will be seen as the valuable kingdom asset that God intended it to be, shaping and changing the world around us with great effect.

This book, *Aligning with the Apostolic*, serves as a spiritual parallel to the "Library of Congress," a provision of important literary works that are forever archived to serve as a reference for how we function and flow as the human race. Thank God for Dr. Cook and each of the contributing writers for this timely treasure.

Dr. Gordon E. Bradshaw

President/Governing Apostle - Global Effect Movers & Shakers Network (GEMS)

President -The "ACT-ivity" Institute Center for Kingdom Empowerment

Author - The Technology of Apostolic Succession: Transferring the Purposes of God to the Next Generation of Kingdom Citizens

Author - Authority for Assignment: Releasing the Mantle of God's Government in the Marketplace

www.GEMSNETWORK.org

FOREWORD BY
DR. BILL HAMON

Bruce Cook has blessed the Body of Christ by presenting an in-depth study of the ascension gift ministry of the Apostle.

The Church was founded on the ministry of the Apostles and Prophets. The first 300 years of the Church, the ministry of the Apostle and Prophet were accepted and recognized as valid and essential ministries within the Church. However, during the Dark Age of the Church, when the formal dead works Church was the only representative of Christianity, the five-fold ministry of the Church was changed to Pope, Cardinals, Bishop, Fathers, Priest, etc.

In 1500, God began the period of the great restoration of the Church. Each of the restoration movements restarted more New Testament truth back into the Church. However, it was not until the Prophetic-Apostolic Movement in the 1980's-90's that the restoration of Prophets and Apostles took place within the Church. I was privileged to pioneer the restoration of Prophets and Prophetic ministry in the 1980's and wrote three books on the prophets and prophetic ministry. Then in the 1990's, I helped pioneer the restoration of Apostles along with other men and women of God. In 1997 I wrote the book on "Apostles and Prophets." It was one of the first books published on the restoration of Apostles. Now numerous books have been written.

Bruce Cook has now pulled together many of these teachings to give a broad and balanced understanding of the Apostle. His works will bless the Church for years to come. God bless you Bruce, for your vision and work to establish the Apostle more freely within Christ's Church.

Apostle/Dr. Bill Hamon

Bishop: Christian International Ministries Network (CIMN),
Christian International Apostolic Network (CIAN)
Christian International Global Network (CIGN)

Author of many books such as *Day Of The Saints*
and *The 3rd and Final Church Reformation*

www.christianinternational.com

SECTION IV:

APOSTOLIC
INTERCESSION

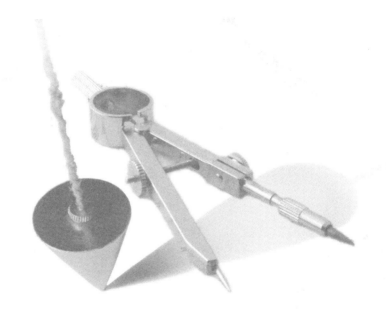

CHAPTER TWENTY-FOUR

APOSTOLIC-PROPHETIC INTERCESSORS

DR. TOMMI FEMRITE

Workplace leaders and CEOs around the world are discovering the value of inviting the presence and power of God into their workplace. This is accomplished in part by embracing corporate and personal intercessors. However, once these leaders have made the decision to invite and increase God's presence by incorporating intercession in their business, finding and equipping those intercessors can be a challenge.

THE KINGDOM OF GOD ENCOMPASSES THE WHOLE WORLD

Intercessors stand in the gap for people, situations, and lands. It is time we shift the way we pray to change society. As Ezek. 22:30-31 says, *"And I searched for a man among them who should build up the wall and stand in the gap before Me for the land, that I should not destroy it; but I found no one. Thus I have poured out My indignation on them; I have consumed them with the fire of My wrath; their way I have brought upon their heads,' declares the Lord GOD"* (NAS). When God looks for someone to stand in the gap and intercede, will He find you? Someone has to war. Someone has to be the voice.

Someone is going to hear from Heaven; it might as well be you or me.

We, as apostolic-prophetic intercessors, are called to stand in the gap. However, most people do not pray for those in the workplace because they do not know what to pray. Many Christians think money is dirty. We even refer to people as being filthy rich. The majority of churches minister to the family (kids, teens, the elderly). What about the workplace? Nearly all workplace people would not call the church if they had trouble with their business. They feel guilty about using the church leader's time or they do not trust those who pray.

APOSTOLIC-PROPHETIC INTERCESSORS LINK WITH FIVE-FOLD MINISTRY

"And He gave some as apostles, and some as prophets, and some as evangelists, and some as pastors and teachers" (Eph. 4:11, NAS). God is raising up cutting-edge networks that link apostles, prophets, pastors, teachers, evangelists, and other workplace leaders with apostolic intercessors. In doing so, these apostles and leaders are empowered to strategically fulfill their destiny, resulting in the transformation of society.

These intercessors embrace a spirit of excellence as they provide apostolic-prophetic intercession for apostles and other leaders in the workplace, thereby empowering them to strategically fulfill their destiny, resulting in the transformation of society. They function in two ways: connecting leaders in the workplace with apostolic intercessors and connecting apostolic intercessors with leaders, thereby enhancing the relationship between the two groups. We must recognize that the five-fold ministry gifts are not limited to the nuclear church, but are designed by God to function in every area of society to include family, church, education, media, arts & entertainment, government and business.

It is time to fight and take back the Seven Mountains of Influence, but a task of such magnitude cannot be accomplished without prayer. Workplace influencers on these Seven Mountains NEED powerful, purposeful intercessors. Prayers will always be a tremendous asset and make a significant difference in what is accomplished. It is important to realize that God places intercessors strategically in the right place at the right time to pray so His kingdom comes and His will is done in the Seven Mountains.

I am always amazed how the Lord orchestrates circumstances and puts people in the right place at the right time so they can accomplish His purposes and plans for His kingdom. In 2000, I was leading intercession for Ed Silvoso's Harvest Evangelism meetings in Argentina. A visiting pastor from Singapore, whom I had met in Texas years prior, was attending the event. He shared his concern about a couple in his church who were in the oil and gas business. They desperately needed prayer and he asked me to commit to praying for them.

Something clicked inside of me and I knew I was to pray for this couple, even though I had never met or spoken to them. My prayer assignment from the Lord began. Eight months later when I was ministering in Texas, we arranged to meet for the first time. During lunch, I shared the different points I had been praying about and the way I prayed for them. Kevin and Colleen (not their real names) were quite surprised that I "looked normal, acted normal, and spoke normal." They decided it would "work" for me to continue to pray for them.

As time passed, our relationship grew and trust developed. One day Kevin called and asked me to pray for his company and partners. Operations had not been going well in the company for about 18 months. The head partner was operating unethically, cheating and working the books. Kevin and two other partners, both very strong Christians, were extremely concerned about the situation. They asked me to pray so they would know what to do. I prayed they would take a stand for righteousness and truth, do what was morally right without compromising, and be obedient to do what God had called them to do. The three men got together and decided, "Okay, we are all resigning. We are beginning our own company founded on Christian principles and we are going to operate under these principles."

Intercession helped these three men make a difficult but correct business decision. It gave them courage to make the change immediately. They made the break from the company and broke through into a new place! The three started their own oil and gas company which was founded and operated on godly principles. They even wrote a vision and mission statement based on the Lord's guidance:

Mission: We are an association of people brought together for the glory of the Kingdom of God who gives us power to create wealth from the treasures of oil, gas and other resources of the earth to advance the purposes of God in the Earth Realm.

Vision: With God working through our expertise, gifts and faith, we will co-labor to bring hope and transformation to our world.

WEAK LINK OR MISSING LINI

Think of a chain. It has often been said, "You are only as strong as your weakest link." Perhaps the weakest link or missing link of workplace influencers on these Seven Mountains is intercession. It is time they get the spiritual protection they need for breakthrough to the next level without all the attacks from the enemy. Intercessors come alongside workplace influencers as Aarons and Hurs who lift up their arms so they can carry out their assignment with remarkable, extraordinary success. *"But Moses' hands were heavy. Then they took a stone and put it under him, and he sat on it; and Aaron and Hur supported his hands, one on one side and one on the other. Thus his hands were steady until the sun set"* (Ex. 17:12, NAS).

It is amazing the number of people in the workplace who do not have a personal prayer shield. They may have a friend, spouse, or co-worker who prays for them, but even these may not be as effective as they need to be. Perhaps they do not trust people who pray (intercessors). Maybe they do not know what a prayer shield or prayer team is, or what it should look like. They could be wondering how to develop a prayer team. They might even ask themselves, "What should I do when I am still experiencing attacks and it seems as though my prayer shield is not working?"

It is time for them to let their intercessors fight alongside them so they have the time and energy to hear from God on how to lead their organization more effectively. Intercession makes the difference! God has intercessors for those in the workplace. All they need to do is connect with them.

APOSTOLIC-PROPHETIC INTERCESSORS

Apostolic/prophetic intercessors may be the missing link in taking their mountain for the Lord. The first question most people ask is, "What is apostolic intercession?" Apostolic intercession consists of making proclamations, declarations, and decrees that are released with the objective of unlocking God's Kingdom purposes on Earth. This sounds exciting, but what do these words actually mean?

God is calling us to shift the way we think. Will you agree with what God says about you? If not, then you will not be able to pray like God called you to pray, nor will you be able to receive prayer. When God says it is time to shift, how are you going to reply?

God is also calling us to shift the way we pray. We shift from giving God all the information He already knows. We shift from making announcements, giving reports or information in our prayers. We shift from asking God to do what He has already said He will do!

God is also calling us to shift the way we intercede. We shift from petition, which means asking God for something. What is wrong with these petition prayers? NOTHING! But, our prayers can be more powerful. I've heard people pray, "God, we ask that we can come boldly before Your throne." But Heb. 4:16 reads, *"Let us therefore come boldly unto the throne of grace, that we may obtain mercy, and find grace to help in time of need"* (KJV). Many times I hear people pray at the beginning of a meeting, "God, we ask for Your presence to come." But, Matt. 18:20 reads, *"For where two or three have gathered together in My name, there I am in their midst"* (NASB).

SHIFT FROM PETITION TO PROCLAMATIONS, DECLARATIONS, AND LEGISLATING DECREES

To help you out, here are some simple definitions of different types of prayer:

Declaration: *To officially pronounce with authority.*

Decree: *A formal order having the force of law, a judicial decision or order, one of the eternal purposes of God, to command, ordain, or decide by, or as if by decree.*

Intercede: *To stand in prayer on behalf of a person, situation, or land.*

Legislate: *To make or enact a law.*

Proclamation: *To officially announce and make known publically.*

Prophetic: *To say what God says.*

Prophetic declaration: *To officially pronounce with authority what God says.*

Prophetic proclamation: *To officially announce and make known publically what God says.*

Speaking forth God's intended will for Earth carries great power to perform His intended purpose. Words of authority spoken in faith and boldness release things that are in the Father's heart but are not yet visible on Earth. Believers have the authority to create God's will on Earth through words of proclamation and decrees that cause God's already existing will to be released. Godly proclamations and declarations are not just words spoken into the air or written on a piece of paper. They are used to stop the evil purposes of the enemy and to release the blessings of God.

Proclamations, declarations, and decrees are weapons of warfare designed by the Lord to destroy onslaughts of wicked spirits. Believers speak words of power and authority as they decree the will of God. First we have to discern the will of God through the Word and the Spirit. It is important for us to know there are three powerful results. Evil powers are rendered powerless. Faith is released to the hearers of the proclamation or decree. God's will and blessings are released on Earth.[1]

Prophetic Proclamation means to speak out loud, to officially announce to the heavenly hosts, to the kingdom of light and to the kingdom of darkness and to a situation, person, nation, land, business, etc. Know which word to use. You represent the voice of the Lord. Remind the enemy of his defeat; remind the Lord of His promises. Call things not as they are but as they should be. Remember that God's Word does not return void; it stands forever.

When God releases a decree, it causes a shift to happen in the heavens and sets events in motion in the Earth. An unseen force begins to move things in a certain direction to fulfill the divine decree. Sometimes the fulfillment comes instantaneously. When God spoke and decreed the worlds and the universe to be formed, instantly, out of nothing, creation took place. Not all decrees are fulfilled instantaneously. God decreed that Abraham would bring forth nations out of his loins and that they would rise up and take the land from the Nile to the Euphrates (Gen. 22:17-18).[2]

The Religious Spirit will try to hold us back from shifting. Dan. 7:25 reveals the strategy of the enemy: *"And he will speak out against the Most High and wear down the saints of the Highest One, and he will intend to make alterations in times and in law; and they will be given into his hand for a time, times, and half a time"* (NASB). It will hinder or wear out shifting and interceding.

APOSTOLIC STRATEGIES

Apostolic/prophetic intercessors are those who shift from asking God to do things to officially announcing, declaring, and decreeing what God has promised He will do. These commanding actions are released with great faith by the intercessors. They know what is spoken will be manifested on Earth. Apostolic intercessors implement apostolic strategies for those in the workplace and war in apostolic intercession for the transference of wealth.

> *"The weapons we fight with are not the weapons of the world. On the contrary, they have divine power to demolish strongholds."*
> (2 Cor. 10:4, NASB)

To shift our nation back to our godly values and purpose, we must invade the Seven Mountains of Society. The word invade is not a very big word, but the meaning has tremendous power. Invade means to enter forcefully as an enemy; go into with hostile intent; to enter as if to take possession; to enter and cause injury or destruction. Destruction means to destroy, demolish, and absolutely annihilate the enemy. How do we invade? We intrude and enter without invitation, permission, or welcome. We advance beyond established limits of property, dominion, or rights of another with the purpose of possessing the land. We do this gradually and often stealthily so that our new foundation is barely noticed. We penetrate, permeate, and influence the affairs of those in control. We invade as an army whose assignment is to possess and overrun the enemy.

We war with words from our mouth by saying what the Lord says. Our words are our weapons.

PROCLAMATIONS, DECLARATIONS AND DECREES

One specific area where a lot of people struggle with praying confidently is finances. When it comes to praying for finances, many of us are in a quandary as to how to actually do this. We wonder if our prayers are in agreement with the Lord's will, what to pray, how to ask God, and how to get breakthroughs.

God is bound by His Word to honor His Word. There is a tremendous amount of power and authority in the scriptures. I discovered that when I pray the scriptures, answers come. Therefore, I have compiled some scriptures and written them in prayer form to pray for wealth and prosperity. You will see that I have shifted from asking God to do things, to making proclamations, declarations, and decrees.

You can pray these prayers below for yourself, for your family, friends, church, business, co-workers, and even clients. All you have to do is fill in the blank with the name of the person you are praying for and declare breakthroughs on their behalf. I am standing with you for wealth and prosperity.

SCRIPTURAL PRAYERS FOR PROSPERITY

I declare wealth and honor comes from the Lord. God is the ruler of all things. In His hands are strength and power to exalt and give strength to _____. (1 Chron. 29:12)

I proclaim _____ is blessed because he/she fears the Lord and he/she finds great delight in God's commands. _____'s children will be mighty in the land. Wealth and riches are in _____'s house. _____'s righteousness endures forever. Even when darkness tries to overtake _____, light will come bursting in. I declare _____ is kind and merciful and all goes well for him/her because he/she is a generous man/woman who conducts his/her business fairly. I decree _____ will not be overcome by evil circumstances. God's constant care of him/her will make a deep impression on all who see it. I declare _____ does not fear bad news or live in dread of what may happen. _____ is settled in his/her mind that Jehovah will take care of him/her, and that is why _____ is not afraid and can calmly face his/her foes. _____ gives generously to those in need. His/her deeds will never be forgotten. He/she shall have influence and honor. I proclaim evil-minded men will be infuriated when they see all this; they will gnash their teeth in anger and slink away, their hopes thwarted. (Ps. 112:1-10, TLB)

I proclaim it is the Lord God who gives _____ the power to become rich. God does this to fulfill His promise to _____'s ancestors. (Deut. 8:18)

I decree the power of the wicked will be broken. I declare the Lord upholds _____ because he/she is righteous. Day by day the Lord observes the good deeds done by _____ and gives him/her eternal rewards. I proclaim God cares for _____ when times are hard; even in famine, _____ will have enough. (Ps. 37:17-18, TLB)

I declare _____ is filled with happiness and joy because he/she does not follow evil men's advice. _____ does not hang around with sinners scoffing at the things of God. _____ delights in doing everything God wants him/her to do. Day and night _____ meditates on God's laws and thinks about ways to follow God more closely. I proclaim _____ is like a tree along a riverbank bearing luscious fruit each season without fail. His/her leaves shall never wither and all he/she does shall prosper. (Ps. 1:1-3, TLB)

I declare Jehovah God is _____'s Light and Protector. He gives _____ grace and glory. No good thing will the Lord withhold from _____ because he/she walks along God's paths. (Ps. 84:11, TLB)

I decree _____ will be made rich in every way so that he/she can be generous on every occasion. _____'s generosity will result in others giving thanksgiving to God. (2 Cor. 9:11, NIV)

I proclaim that _____, who is uncompromisingly righteous, shall flourish like the palm tree. He/she will be long-lived, stately, upright, useful, and fruitful. _____ shall grow like a cedar in Lebanon that is majestic, stable, durable, and incorruptible. I declare _____ is planted in the house of the Lord. He/she shall flourish in the courts of our God. As _____ grows in grace, he/she shall still bring forth fruit in old age. I proclaim _____ shall be full of sap, of spiritual vitality, and rich in the verdure of trust, love, and contentment. _____ is a living memorial to show that the Lord is upright and faithful to His promises. I decree the Lord is _____'s Rock, and there is no unrighteousness in Him. (Ps. 92:12-15, AMP)

I declare that _____ is a generous man/woman who will prosper. As he/she refreshes others, he/she will be refreshed. (Prov. 11:25, NIV)

OVERCOMING FEAR IN THE MIDST OF ECONOMIC CRISIS

Fear is working overtime in many of us. Listening to the media and reading the newspaper waters our fears on a regular basis and causes it to grow. All of us are afraid sometimes; that is normal. However, some of us are fearful most of the time and that is not normal. We must learn to overcome our fears so that we can pray more effectively against the fears that are assaulting us and leaders.

Satan is the source of fear. Fear is one of Satan's main strategies for immobilizing God's workers. Satan is the master of scare tactics and fear is an enemy to faith. We combat fear with positive faith in the Word of God to gain and promote a reverence for the Lord.

The fears of life consist of the fear of being hurt, rejected, persecuted, and abandoned. It encompasses the fear of lack—not having enough, going bankrupt, making a mistake, showing imperfections, or failing as a person. We fear things, places, people, social interaction, rejection, anger, disapproval, failure, success, thoughts, economic crisis, the unknown, death, and fear itself. Fear is a powerful, negative driving force. However, hope is a powerful, positive, driving force.

We each have different ways that we keep our fears alive. Some avoid facing their fears while others run away from them. Some think fearful thoughts and then exaggerate it to the worst, while some enlist the help of others as a cushion against fear. Some are consumed by fear while others keep theirs totally hidden. A couple of phrases that cause us to approach fear from a position of weakness are: I can't...That's a problem...I'll never...That's awful...What if...I should...Why is life this way?...If only...Life is a big struggle...What will I do?

The good news is we can live our life free from fear even during an economic crisis. Fear can ruin our life, so we need to know how to overcome it. Fear is a liar. It says, "God can't!" Fear is irrational especially if we know God. A good dose of truth will dissolve most fears immediately. Other fears may take a little longer, but they too will go. Fear can be conquered!

A common trap of the enemy is allowing fear to paralyze us so we cannot think or process clearly. Perhaps we listen to those around us who are afraid, or we listen to the media or read the papers regarding financial crisis. The advice of ungodly people is often based on fear. The passive mind accepts fear and allows its fantasies to spread unchecked. Fear paints a devastated future while faith erases the lies and causes us to see the best days ahead of us.

God can replace our fear with courage. We must spend time with Him to learn what He wants and catch His attitude toward the situation. Often you have heard people say, "I'm scared to death," or, "I always get nervous when I have to speak in front of a group," or, "I never sleep well the night before I start a new job." Perhaps you say the same things. Reject such thinking and stop fanning the fire of fear. Facts tend to change a person's viewpoint. Listen to the truth and act accordingly. This is step one in conquering fear. We must defeat fear with fact. We must learn to tell ourselves the truth—the truth that God is all powerful.

Instead of worrying or being afraid, set aside time to be alone with God. Whenever our focus slips from God to us, we are in for instant trouble. One way to keep our focus on God when fear threatens to smother our faith is to remember with joy and thankfulness what God has done and how He has helped us in the past. Then receive His power for our present situation and expect miracles. Fear is irrational and tends to overpower clear thinking. Do a Bible study on fear. Look up the 366 "Fear nots." God gives us the hope we need when He says, "Fear not." We can ask the Holy Spirit to apply this hope to our situation.

Fear is atheistic; it leaves God out. Sometimes evil seems so overwhelming that it frightens us or our clients, silences us or demoralizes us, thus crippling our ability to live for Jesus. Instead, we need to face evil squarely and let God deal with the situation. We gain confidence by praying—including praying in the Spirit. And, we realize that God will deal with evil because He has all power and will defeat evil, so we do not have to be afraid. When evil comes our way, we can take God's hand, knowing He can conquer all the forces of Satan.

Perhaps we have trusted God completely for something last year, but this year we are a nervous wreck. GOD HAS NOT CHANGED! So, what is the problem? Yesterday's faith does not automatically cover today's fears. We have to continually stick close to Jesus, constantly renew our mind by letting the Word speak to us, and daily receive the power of the Holy Spirit. Faith remembers what fear forgets. In order to walk in faith, we need to know exactly where we stand with the Lord.

"God has not given us a spirit of fear" (2 Tim. 1:7, NASB). So, we must admit that fear comes from the very gates of Hell.

We cannot be overthrown by fear, anxiety and worry if we are in a right relationship with the Lord and maturing in it. *"If God be for us, who can stand against us"* (Rom 8:31, NASB). When we really believe that God not only loves us but also is in complete control of us, we begin to feel secure. Only the Word of God brings this out.

It is God's desire that we fear Him. Satan has a counterfeit for everything that is God's. Satan turns the fear (reverence) towards God to fear (terror) towards him. *"I sought the LORD, and He answered me, and delivered me from all my fears"* (Ps. 34:4, NASB). *"There is no fear in love; but perfect love casts out fear, because fear involves punishment, and the one who fears is not perfected in love"* (1 John 4:18, NASB). We need to know the Perfect One who loves perfectly.

SEE YOURSELF AS A VICTORIOUS WARRIOR!

One of the favorite scriptures being quoted today, especially by Christian business leaders and entrepreneurs is Prov. 13:22, *"A good man leaves an inheritance [of moral stability and goodness] to his children's children, and the wealth of the sinner [finds its way eventually] into the hands of the righteous, for whom it was laid up"* (AMP).

Those who are interceding for business leaders and entrepreneurs are doing their best to see this is happening for their clients. At times you may even have found yourself with outstretched hands, looking up to Heaven, waiting for wealth to rain down. Don't laugh! We have all done it at one time or another!

However, as we are all aware, this transference of wealth has not yet begun to happen for many of us in the measure that I believe God is speaking to us in Proverbs. While there can be many reasons for why this is not taking place to the degree that it should, I believe one of the reasons for this lack of God's promise manifesting in the earth is that we fail to recognize this is not only about selling a product or providing a service. It is about a war to see a repositioning of Satan's kingdom's wealth by capturing and placing it into the hands of believing business leaders for God's Kingdom purposes.

In fact, I believe that through scripture we see that this transference of wealth God declares as His desire constitutes spiritual warfare. We see this when Jesus said, *"And from the days of John the Baptist until the present time, the kingdom of heaven has endured violent assault, and violent men seize it by force [as a precious prize--a share in the heavenly kingdom is sought with most ardent zeal and intense exertion]"* (Matt. 11:12, AMP). Therefore, I declare over each intercessor that you are a PRIZE FIGHTER!

In Ezek. 28:13, we see an allegorical picture of Satan. The scripture says that when God created Satan, he was clothed in gold, diamonds, and every precious stone. In other words, he was clothed in wealth. After the fall in the garden, the dominion over everything that had been given to Adam and Eve, including the wealth of the earth, was given over to Satan. Once again, he clothed himself in these riches. Even Jesus did not contest this statement during his trial in the wilderness (Luke 4:6).

When we engage in business for God's Kingdom wealth-building, we are essentially removing Satan's clothing of unrighteous wealth right from off his back! That is why it can be such a struggle to succeed in business; even though we are living righteously and standing in faith for all of the promises of God, we are at war in taking away from Satan what he deceived Adam and Eve into giving him.

Now, all power and dominion has been given to Jesus and the body of Christ, but we apprehend these blessings by faith, spiritual warfare, and action. The fact that we have been given the promises of blessings is not enough to see them manifest. We have to take back the wealth from Satan so that the kingdoms of this world will become the Kingdom of our Lord and His Christ (Rev. 11:15).

Kingdom marketplace intercessors should wake up every day putting on the full armor spoken of in Ephesians 6 to see this promise of God for wealth transfer take place. Realize that we are literally going into battle through our intercession to see that our clients are not overwhelmed by the enemy forces that are trying to keep this promise of God from taking place!

One good example of receiving a promise from God through spiritual warfare is found in the Israelites' struggle to enter the Promised Land. God had already promised He would lead them to the Promised Land that He had already given to them (Gen. 12:7, Ex. 3:8). However, during the journey there, the Amalekites came out to fight them. While Joshua fought the battle on the field (workplace), Moses, Aaron, and Hur fought a spiritual battle (intercession).

Whenever the intercessors succeeded, the army of the Israelites prevailed. When Joshua's intercessors rested, the Israelite army was overpowered by the enemy (Ex. 17:11). Notice that victory always happens in the spiritual realm before it manifests in the natural or workplace realm. It was not enough that God promised that He had given them the Promised Land, or that He would wipe out the Amalekites from the face of the earth. There was still both a spiritual

even though He found the head it for it! gave them the had to pay

and natural battle that needed to take place before the Israelites could walk in the blessings that God promised.

Many Christians are standing on the promises of God with outstretched hands, waiting for Him to deliver. However, just as the Israelites found out when they came to the Promised Land, the land was already occupied by an enemy that was bigger and stronger. Although God gave it to them, He expected them to receive it through warfare. As Jesus said, *"The kingdom of heaven suffers violence, and violent men take it by force"* (Matt. 11:12). This is where you and I do our warfare in our intercession.

Daniel was a type of business intercessor for a king. He was considered a "wise man" and had an excellent spirit in him. Daniel was seeking revelation from God on a vision he had received. The enemy tried to prevent Daniel from receiving his answer. There was a spiritual battle in the heavens for 21 days during which time Daniel fasted and prayed. At the end of the 21 days, there was breakthrough in the spirit realm; and after that, there was a breakthrough in the natural realm (Dan. 10:12-13). Note in verse 12 that God had granted Daniel his request on the first day, but it took 21 days of spiritual battle before Daniel could see a manifestation of results in the natural realm. We need to remember this! *Yes Lord!*

The battle is always won in the spirit realm before the victory (or wealth) manifests in the natural realm. The enemy of our souls is a seasoned general with an army of warriors (demons), and he has no intention of giving up what he perceives to be his wealth without a fight. One of our missions as intercessors is to manifest the Kingdom of God on earth by taking possession and dominion of the occupied spiritual territories that are currently controlled by the enemy in the workplace. God told Adam and Eve to take dominion and subdue it (Gen. 1:8). That command in the Church age has not changed. As intercessors, we are called to go into the Promised Land (workplace) and take dominion away from the enemy so that the kingdoms of this world will become the Kingdoms of our Lord Jesus.

As we seek to assist our clients to take dominion of their respective spheres through our intercession, I believe some business battles will not be won without a Daniel anointing, which combines fasting with our intercession. Most business leaders have neither the time nor experience to spend days or even weeks fasting and praying for a breakthrough. Dedicated workplace intercessors can help them fight this battle in the spiritual realm, while the business leaders fight the battle on the field (or in the board room).

CONCLUSION

The apostolic movement in the marketplace is only increasing, just as His kingdom is only ever increasing. Prayer—proclamation, declaration, and decree—is absolutely needed for us to have successful kingdom businesses.

Begin to set aside just a few minutes every day to make proclamations and declarations over your business. Ask God to bring intercessors to you who will commit to faithfully cover your business and relationships in prayer. Then watch out, because you are about to break through to a whole new level of success.

ENDNOTES

1. Barbara Wentroble, *Praying with Authority*, pp. 124, 127, 130-133. Ventura, CA: Regal Books, 2003.
2. Jane Hamon, *The Cyrus Decree*, pp. 89-90. Santa Rosa Beach, FL: Christian International Ministries, 2001.

ABOUT THE AUTHOR

Tommi Femrite is founding apostle of GateKeepers International and Apostolic Intercessors Network. Tommi is recognized as a spiritual strategist who is able to assess the enemy's grip, receive God's strategic battle plans and communicate these plans to leaders with great precision. Highly respected as a teacher, she couples the wisdom of God with her heart-warming sense of humor.

Tommi is an author, an ordained minister, has earned a Doctorate of Practical Ministry from Wagner Leadership Institute and is a member of the International Coalition of Apostles and the Eagles' Vision Apostolic Team.

Tommi and her husband, Ralph, live in Colorado Springs, Colo. They have two adult children and four grandchildren. For 30 years, Ralph and Tommi have ministered around the world. Their three decades of service and ministry have taken them into the hearts of thousands in Europe, Asia, Africa, Australia, North America and South America. To learn more or contact her, visit her web sites at www. gatekeepersintl.org or www.AIN-GKI.org.

CHAPTER TWENTY-FIVE

THE SPIRITUAL ARCHITECT

TIM TAYLOR

"For we are God's fellow workers; you are God's field, you are God's building. According to the grace of God which was given to me, as a wise master builder I have laid the foundation, and another builds on it. But let each one take heed how he builds on it. For no other foundation can anyone lay than that which is laid, which is Jesus Christ."
(1 Cor. 3:9-11, NKJV)

Paul the apostle is the one who penned this portion of scripture which provides keen insight into another aspect of the apostolic gift, its role and its order. He describes himself as a "master builder." The Greek word *architekton* translated "master builder" literally means chief architect. Architects are the first ones to work on a project and design plans which move a structure from vision into reality. These plans provide the pattern from which the general contractor and all of the sub-contractors work from.

This is why in 1 Cor. 12:28 apostles go first, prophets second and teachers third. It is an order of function. God has uniquely designed this gift with revelation and wisdom to build. This gift working with the prophet lays the foundation for all of the rest of the gifts to successfully build their part while interacting with the rest of the team.

PLANS BY THE SPIRIT

> *"Then David gave his son Solomon the plans for the vestibule, its houses, its treasuries, its upper chambers, its inner chambers, and the place of the mercy seat; and the plans for all that he had by the Spirit, of the courts of the house of the Lord, of all the chambers all around, of the treasuries of the house of God, and of the treasuries for the dedicated things."*
> (1 Chron. 28:11-12, NKJV)

God gave King David plans by the spirit of God. The king served as an architect, taking the vision for a house or dwelling place for the Lord and turning that into a set of plans from which his son and a very large team of builders could work from. He built a structure that had never existed and its very design introduces some intriguing questions.

How was he able to do this?

Why was there a need for treasuries?

How was David able to get these plans by the Spirit?

> *"'After! this I will return and will rebuild the tabernacle of David, which has fallen down; I will rebuild its ruins, and I will set it up; So that the rest of mankind may seek the Lord, even all the Gentiles who are called by My name,' says the Lord who does all these things."*
> (Acts 15:16-17, NKJV)

King David was a type of forerunner to the apostolic gift. He was from the tribe of Judah (praise) and he served as a king, acted like a prophet and interceded like a priest in his generation. Once he was set in as the king, the first decision he and his leaders made was to bring back the presence of God to his city, the capitol of his kingdom. Why?

David's kingdom was made up of people from every sphere of society. His concern was not for his own well-being but for the Lord's glory, His will, and the well-being and success of the people David was given responsibility for. David was concerned about laying a good solid foundation for each of the tribes and families to be successful in their respective professions and callings.

> *"'Since the day that I brought My people Israel out of Egypt,*
> *I have chosen no city from any tribe of Israel in which*
> *to build a house, that My name might be there;*
> *but I chose David to be over My people Israel.'*
> *Now it was in the heart of my father David to build*
> *a temple for the name of the Lord God of Israel."*
> (1 Kings 8:16-18, NKJV)

The vision for Solomon's temple came out of David's heart. It was his vision. He dreamed and by working with our Lord, he created. This is a great way to build relationship. Candidly, I've found I get to know people better and faster when I work with them than I ever do just fellowshipping over a meal. Think about how much the Lord loves to work with each of us on our assignments. God created us in His image and that is why He gave us the ability to dream and envision. He wants us to create, too. He just wants us to consult with Him because He loves us and wants to spend time with us. He wants us to build together with Him like David did.

David, being a forerunner to the apostolic gift, was also an architect. He got the plans by the Spirit. The plans He gave to Solomon were not his first plans by the spirit. I believe the first plans were actually the pattern God showed David on how to welcome God's abiding presence in the city of David. It is referred to in Acts 15:16. It is the restoration of David's tabernacle.

Jesus began his ministry preaching the gospel of the kingdom. His Bible of the day was what we call the Old Testament and King David provided the best example of building the kingdom! We can learn much about God's pattern for expanding the kingdom today by studying what David did when He began to build the kingdom. But before we look at the pattern David set, let's look at why the Spirit led David to design treasuries in the plans he gave to Solomon.

WHY DID DAVID DESIGN TREASURIES INTO SOLOMON'S TEMPLE?

As a king, David had responsibility for how all of the spheres of society connected and interacted. I believe the Seven Mountain concept is like a modern-day parable. It helps us to understand an aspect or a certain view of the kingdom God wants His people to establish.

The first decision King David made to begin to expand the kingdom was to set up a tent on Mount Zion and he established an administration of teams to ensure that God's abiding presence was always welcome in his city. After this was established we see all through 2 Samuel and 1 Chronicles that David's armies saw victory after victory. They acquired spoil from these victories.

It is important to understand that King David was also a skillful general. He had learned the art of war. This skill is also an aspect of the apostolic gift. Here are a couple of excerpts from *Developing Apostolic Strategy* that will shed some light on this aspect of the apostolic gift.

The word apostle was first a Greek/Phoenician seafaring term that meant leader of a convoy of ships. Later it came to refer to the commander of an invasion force. As time went on the Romans used it to refer to former generals who then became ambassadors. The Jewish culture eventually began to use it when speaking of an envoy who collected tribute. Finally, Jesus used it in speaking of the first 12 disciples. In summary, the history of the word meant:

- The leader of a convoy of ships
- The commander of an invasion force
- An ambassador general sent to represent a government to another nation[1]

2 Cor. 10:3-4 says, *"For though we walk in the flesh, we do not war according to the flesh. For the weapons of our warfare are not carnal but mighty in God for pulling down strongholds..."*

The word "war" in the Greek means to serve in a military campaign and to "execute the apostolate." Apostolate literally means the office of apostle. The word warfare in the Greek means "apostolic career" or "strategy." Hence, one of the primary functions of the apostolic gift is spiritual warfare. God made people with this gift to develop strategy.[2]

King David was a skilled general and he knew the importance of taking the high ground. It gave him and his troops a military advantage. As armies win wars and establish justice and righteousness, peace follows; with peace comes prosperity for all areas of society.

So, why did David include treasuries into the design? First, he had experience with his tabernacle. He knew the spiritual, strategic, practical and actual advantage God's abiding presence gave him and his people. It set them up to prosper and be successful. Second, he knew how important tithes and offerings were in worship.

David loved God's presence and understood the power of prayer, praise and worship. That is why the process to establish a place for God's abiding presence in the City of David began with offerings before they even arrived on Mount Zion. They took six steps toward Zion and began to offer offerings, then David began dancing (2 Sam. 6:13-14). This set the Levites up to do their job! Their job was to steward and ensure that continual prayer, praise and worship went up every day all day. This was critical to the success of everyone else.

King David amassed a fortune and so did many others. His generosity toward the house of the Lord was one of the keys to his success. David said in 1 Chron. 29:16, *"O Lord our God, all this abundance that we have prepared to build You a house for Your holy name is from Your hand, and is all Your own"* (NKJV). The abundance he acquired was actually God's. God put it in his stewardship and David acknowledged that everything he and his people had acquired, all belonged to God.

Each of us has a call in one of the Seven Mountains. If we neglect God's house then we can expect God to send a drought on our mountains.

"'You looked for much, but indeed it came to little; and when you brought it home, I blew it away. Why?' says the Lord of hosts. 'Because of My house that is in ruins, while every one

of you runs to his own house. Therefore the heavens above
you withhold the dew, and the earth withholds its fruit.
For I called for a drought on the land and the mountains,
on the grain and the new wine and the oil, on whatever the
ground brings forth, on men and livestock,
and on all the labor of your hands.'"
(Hag. 1:9-11, NKJV)

THE MOUNTAIN OF THE LORD'S HOUSE

King David was a wise military commander as well as a
spiritual architect. He knew the advantage of taking the
high ground. David knew that the key to success in the
Seven Mountains was to first occupy the mountain of the
Lord's house whose pattern is found on Mount Zion.

"Now it shall come to pass in the latter days that the
mountain of the Lord's house shall be established on the top
of the mountains, and shall be exalted above the hills; And
all nations shall flow to it. Many people shall come and say,
'Come, and let us go up to the mountain of the Lord, to the
house of the God of Jacob; He will teach us His ways, and we
shall walk in His paths,' for out of Zion shall go forth the law,
and the word of the Lord from Jerusalem."
(Isa. 2:2-3, NKJV)

What occurred on Mount Zion in the tabernacle of David?
David asked the Levites to steward 24/7 prayer, praise
and worship. One of the functions of a king is to establish
systems of administration. Show me a king or a government
without an administration and I'll show you a government
that exists only as a fantasy of the mind.

David empowered the Levites to fulfill their assigned
call. David understood the truth expressed in Eph. 4:16

which teaches us that when every part does its share, it causes the body to edify itself in love. David's success was interconnected with others. It was to his benefit to see the Levites fulfill what our Lord had called them to do. This mountain is the location of the Lord's house of prayer for all nations.

> *"Even them I will bring to My holy mountain, and make them joyful in My house of prayer. Their burnt offerings and their sacrifices will be accepted on My altar; for My house shall be called a house of prayer for all nations."*
> (Isa. 56:7, NKJV)

The tithes and offerings belong to God and are a critical part of worship and important signs of our trust in our Lord's covenantal promises. Truly the lesser is blessed by the better (Heb. 7:4-10). David the king ensured that our Lord and the Levites received what they needed to ensure God's abiding presence was continually welcome in the capitol city.

The emphasis in the tabernacle of David was not the physical structure. The emphasis was on the administration and management of people to ensure that 24/7 prayer, praise and worship went up continually. David ensured that an honorable distribution system was in place to ensure the Levites could perform the service he requested of them. This is what occurred on Mount Zion.

Every one of the Seven Mountains has a form of wealth but the business mountain is certainly the most prominent when it comes to the acquisition of financial abundance and resources. It is a spiritual war that requires divine wisdom and strategy.

"What will they answer the messengers of the nation?
That the Lord has founded Zion, and the poor of
His people shall take refuge in it."
(Isa. 14:32, NKJV)

The Lord "founded" Zion. The Hebrew word translated founded means to sit down together and consult. This provides keen insight into the wisdom God gave David. In 1 Chron. 11, all the leaders gathered together to make one person king and that was David. David was responsible for all of society and I don't think he knew everything. I believe he formed councils of leaders in every sphere of society just like he taught his son Solomon (Prov. 24:3-6).

Personally, I believe that David understood that God was the Spirit of wisdom, understanding, counsel and might (Isa. 11:1-2). I believe that he assigned the Levites the task of stewarding the 24/7 in his city because David wanted the Spirit of wisdom, understanding, counsel and might in the presence of his councils.

In response to David's desire, God gave David a spiritual architectural plan which he implemented in the tabernacle of David. This is a pattern God gave David and this is how the Lord "founded" Zion. God wants to sit with us and provide us counsel. He wants to share with us divine plans to build wealth and apostolic strategies to overcome the schemes of the enemy and set people free. He wants us to be His steward of kingdom-minded solutions on earth. The continual canopy of prayer, praise and worship opened the windows of heaven such that divine resources, wisdom, miracles and power flowed. As divine wisdom, plans and strategies were acquired, people were sent to practically engage every sphere of society. Prayer led to strategic action combined with wisdom.

This expansion of the kingdom resulted in military victory after military victory. David set his son and the next generation up to live and build in a time of peace such that King Solomon made silver and gold as common as stones (2 Chron. 1:15).

The first mountain we must occupy in our quest to reach the summit of each of the Seven Mountains is the mountain of the Lord's house of prayer for all nations. It is the restored tabernacle of David. It performs the role that the air force provides an army today. It provides the army of the Lord air (prayer) superiority as they engage the prince of the power of the air. It is like the beachhead or base of operations for any strategic engagement. It is the key to the harvest, abundance and success on every mountain.

> "'On that day I will raise up the tabernacle of David, which has fallen down, and repair its damages; I will raise up its ruins, and rebuild it as in the days of old; That they may possess the remnant of Edom, and all the Gentiles who are called by My name,' says the Lord who does this thing. 'Behold, the days are coming,' says the Lord, 'When the plowman shall overtake the reaper, and the treader of grapes him who sows seed; The mountains shall drip with sweet wine, and all the hills shall flow with it.'"
> (Amos 9:11-13, NKJV)

THE NEW WINESKIN IS AN ANCIENT PATTERN

We are in the process of building a new wineskin. The truth is, the new wineskin is not really new. It is just new to us. The new wineskin is an ancient pattern. The key to taking the Promised Land and the key to David's kingdom was the Ark of the Covenant. It was where the presence of God rested.

The Lord spoke to me some years ago out of Isa. 4:3-6. It is about how God will visit Mount Zion with a spirit of judgment and burning so that all who remain in Zion will be called holy. It goes on to describe how this will be a place of covering and refuge from the storm. Then this phrase captured my attention in verse 5: *"then the Lord will create above every dwelling place of Mount Zion, and above her assemblies..."* That was when I realized that the Church in any city who did what David did could see a tabernacle of David established in their city.

In 2005 God gave me a strategy to steward that we've been using to assist leaders in taking the first two steps King David took when he began to expand the kingdom. It helps leaders form apostolic (strategic) councils while building 24/7 prayer in a city quickly as local churches each take a day of 24/7 prayer, thereby inviting God's abiding presence into their city and the Spirit of wisdom, understanding, counsel and might into the presence of their councils. That strategy is called Operation Rolling Thunder. It is based upon the pattern the Lord gave King David.

One of the things I've learned about apostolic plans is that God marks "His plans" with supernatural signs and wonders (Heb. 2:4). The word translated as signs in Heb. 2:4 is the Greek word *semion*. It is translated as a sign, wonder or miracle 75 times in God's word except for one time in 2 Thess. 3:17 where the word sign is used in the context of a "signature."

> *"The salutation of Paul with my own hand,*
> *which is a sign in every epistle; so I write."*
> (2 Thess. 3:17, NKJV)

Since 2005 we've recorded over 60+ unusual signs, wonders and miracles in the heavens and on the earth that occurred to mark the delivery of the Lord's strategy or a people engaging God's strategy. Thirty of those signs are recorded in the book *Operation Rolling Thunder Revised*. Let me give you an example of what I mean and then I'll share what the Lord taught me about signs and wonders.

In 2003 Chuck Pierce and Dutch Sheets went on a 50-state tour and prophesied over each state. While in Washington (my state) they prophesied that Alaska was the alpha and omega state because an International Date Line ran through their chain of islands. In 2009 I was invited to present the mobilization strategy Operation Rolling Thunder at Freedom in Christ in North Pole, Alaska.

On the day I landed in Fairbanks, Alaska an undersea volcano erupted. The next day as I presented the strategy to leaders in Fairbanks (mayor, fire chief, business leaders, etc.) and taught them how to form apostolic councils, a 2.2 earthquake was recorded 4.2 miles south-southwest of our location. Two hours after I flew out, Mount Redoubt erupted. This was a volcanic occurrence on the other side of the International Date Line.

Operation Rolling Thunder (ORT) is based on Ps. 18:6-14. King David wrote this Psalm. It is all about the voice of the Lord and the conditions that occur when God's presence shows up and He speaks. He comes with black clouds, lightning, hailstones, fire, the earth shakes and when He speaks His voice is like thunder and it scatters the enemy. So, on the first day I arrived with this message, the earth erupted on one side of the International Date Line. The 2.2 earthquake 4.2 miles south of us marked the primary text that day which was Isa. 2:2 and Mic. 4:1-2 which says, *"in the latter days the mountain of the Lord's house will be established on top of the mountains."* Then Mount Redoubt erupted, marking the end of my trip. The last message I gave included 2 Sam. 5:7 which indicates Zion is a stronghold and Isa. 4:3-6 which teaches that Zion is also a refuge. *Redoubt* is a French word that means stronghold or refuge.

This is what the Lord taught me about signs. Miracles are part of God's signature (sign-nature). Whenever God's people obey the Lord, they write history (His-story) and sometimes He will choose to give a sign as His way of putting His mark on that page of history.

God has put His mark many times on this spiritual architectural plan. It's not my plan; it is my Lord's. Not only have the unusual signs in the heaven and earth followed me, but they have now followed several others who carried the same strategy. This is a mobilization strategy that recognizes three things that are critical to apostolic alignment.

First, God has already deployed apostles and prophets to almost every city. If the Church in each city, made up of many local congregations, would just recognize and receive them, they would be blessed through the operation of their gifts in their assigned territories.

Second, there is wisdom in a multitude of counsel. ORT facilitates the discovery and inventory of gifts in a given city as councils are initially formed representing all Seven Spheres of Society. It becomes a form of gathering the elders at the gates of a city.

Third, it requires the body of Christ, local church by local church, to work together in a city. Most congregations or ministries are too small to facilitate 24/7meetings all year long. ORT has been used to mobilize and strategically unite Kingdom-minded leaders and churches from Catholic to Charismatic and from Presbyterian to Pentecostal, in cities and regions all around the world.

These are spiritual architectural plans given by the spirit of God to help build His house of prayer for all nations. It is a strategy that empowers the Church to occupy the mountain of the Lord's house, giving her air superiority over the prince of the power of the air. It is critical to apostolic alignment and success in the other Seven Mountains. I pray God give you wisdom, courage and revelation, in Jesus' name.

ENDNOTES

1. Tim Taylor, *Developing Apostolic Strategy*, p. 8. Renton, WA: Kingdom League International, 2010.
2. Ibid, p. 9.

ABOUT THE AUTHOR

Tim Taylor is a retired Commander (USNR-ret) recognized as a catalyst, an international leadership trainer, and a strategist who helps leaders put their faith into practical action with measurable results. He is a gifted preacher/ teacher known for his passion and humor. His gift of wisdom, combined with a great love for God's presence, has proven to serve many churches passionate about prayer, transformation, leadership, spiritual warfare and wisdom. Leaders in churches, cities, apostolic networks, businesses and government agencies have asked Tim to consult with their teams to discover strategic solutions. Tim has also authored a number of books which include Operation Rolling Thunder and Developing Apostolic Strategy.

He is the founding apostle of Kingdom League International and is a father and mentor to a number of leaders overseeing churches and city prayer centers in a number of nations. He is the chief architect of Operation Rolling Thunder, a transformation prayer mobilization strategy, that has equipped leaders in over 36 nations to establish 24/7 prayer while forming apostolic councils in all Seven Spheres of Society. To learn more or to contact Tim, visit his websites at www.KingdomLeague.org and www. ORTPrayer.org.

CHAPTER TWENTY-SIX

Title

APOSTOLIC THUNDER: THE SOUND OF THE SONS

JAMES NESBIT

Scripture

"For [even the whole] creation (all nature) waits expectantly and longs earnestly for God's sons to be made known [waits for the revealing, the disclosing of their sonship]."
(Rom. 8:9, AMP)

The whole earth has longed for the era of the apostles into which we have entered. In July 2011, we began to hear from many trusted prophetic voices that at the time of the Feast of Tabernacles in 2011, we would cross over into not just a new season, but a whole new era in the earth.

THE ERA OF HIS PRESENCE

"Believe in the Lord your God and you shall be established; believe and remain steadfast to His prophets and you shall prosper."
(2 Chron. 20:20, AMP)

I believed the words of the prophets, but the question that I kept asking Father God was, "What era are we entering?" While on a 50-day prayer assignment in Chicago between Passover and Pentecost in 2012, I awoke early one morning and clear as a bell I heard, "You have entered the era of My presence."

Scripture

> "And afterward I will pour out My Spirit upon all flesh; and your sons and your daughters shall prophesy, your old men shall dream dreams, your young men shall see visions."
> (Joel 2:28, AMP)

Let's be very clear here! When we enter a new era, everything changes. No matter what things were like in the last era, everything has changed. No matter how thick the darkness, how lost the soul, or how strong the chains, the thunder of His presence destroys the power of darkness. One encounter with the eternal light of the Holy One changes everything; just ask the apostle Paul!

The apostolic sons in the earth today were formed in their mothers' wombs to come to a place in their appointed span of life to move as one with Father, releasing the thunder of the eternal word of the Living God into their spheres of influence on the earth.

The apostolic thunder of the worship, decrees, declarations, and proclamations of these mature sons [sons as used here is a gender-neutral term and includes daughters] releases the light of who He is through the blood of the Lamb. This changes the atmosphere and causes the mountains to tremble and darkness to flee at the presence of the Lord.

RESULTS OF THE RELEASE OF APOSTOLIC THUNDER!

Chicago was given the unfortunate title of "most corrupt" city in America in a new study by the University of Illinois

The Release of Apostolic Thunder

at Chicago and the University of Illinois' Institute of Government and Public Affairs.[1]

Having read this report, I felt we needed to pray for corruption throughout America through the most corrupt city in America.

As regional overseer of six states in mid America for both Apostle John Benefiel, leader of the Heartland Apostolic Prayer Network, and Cindy Jacobs, leader of the United States Reformation Prayer Network, I asked them if we could engage the entire network in focusing on corruption throughout the land by prayer through this Chicago gate.

Another point of focus would be the exposing and removal of corrupt "KINGPINS." One of the things I love about both Apostle Benefiel and Cindy is they want to see tangible results! Listed below are the headlines of newspapers of results released thus far:

Kingpins are coming down—Nationwide raids on synthetic drug labs lead to 90 arrests, seizure of $36 million. In the first-ever nationwide crackdown on the synthetic drug industry, law enforcement officers arrested more than 90 people, seized $36 million in cash and more than 4.8 million packets of synthetic cannabinoids Wednesday, authorities said.[2]

High-Profile Financial Scandals in 5 Months— Corruption continues to be uncovered...exposed... rooted out![3]

Corruption exposed! Illinois House expels Rep. Derrick Smith over bribery charge—State lawmakers today kicked out a West Side Democrat accused of taking a $7,000 bribe, marking the first expulsion from the Illinois House since 1905.[4]

40 people indicted in methamphetamine ring run from Indiana prison—A prison inmate ran a drug ring involving at least three Indiana prisons that sold heroin, methamphetamine and other drugs around the state using cellphones smuggled in by guards, according to a federal indictment unsealed Wednesday that charges 40 people in connection with the scheme.[5]

Study calls for probing of political corruption in more than 60 suburbs June 25, 2012[6].

Corrupt Illinois Lawmaker Exposed—The comptroller of a small city in Illinois is accused of misappropriating more than $30 million in city funds and using the money to support a "lavish lifestyle," including a large farm with over 150 horses, over $339,000 in jewelry, and numerous vehicles. Rita Crundwell, 58, of Dixon, Ill. was arrested on Tuesday by the FBI on a federal charge for stealing more than $3.2 million in public funds since last fall. Authorities, however, believe she had been helping herself to the public funds since 2006.[7]

Chicago—Crime is down dramatically except in 8 neighborhoods[8].

The Occupy Movement Unmasked—7 minute Video[9].

Corruption in LA police uncovered—L.A. suspends 7 cops for 'Jump Out Boys' clique—Seven deputies from the Los Angeles County sheriff's gang unit are on paid leave during an investigation into their suspected involvement in a secret clique that promoted aggressive policing and celebrated officer shootings, sources confirmed to The Los Angeles Times Wednesday[10].

Alleged perpetrator of mass beheadings in Mexico arrested. Mexican soldiers have arrested an alleged perpetrator of the massacre of 49 people whose corpses were decapitated, dismembered and dumped on a highway last week[11].

Joaquin 'El Chapo' Guzman, Mexico's Most-Wanted Drug Lord, Targeted By U.S. Kingpin Act[12].

Last Colombian Drug Kingpin Falls: 'Crazy' Barrera Captured[13].

Mexican navy captures drug kingpin known as 'El Taliban.' Mexican marines have captured a renegade leader of the Zetas known as "El Taliban" in the latest blow by the U.S.-backed commando campaign against the violent gang operating south of the Texas border[14].

LIGHTNING LOOSED, DARKNESS DISPELLED

"The people who walked in darkness have seen a great Light;
those who dwelt in the land of intense darkness and the
shadow of death, upon them has the Light shined."
(Isa. 9:2, AMP)

"See, I have this day appointed you to the oversight of the
nations and of the kingdoms to root out and pull down, to
destroy and to overthrow, to build and to plant."
(Jer. 1:10, AMP)

Not only does the release of apostolic thunder root out, pull down, overthrow and destroy structures of darkness as Jer. 1:10 declares, but it builds and plants as well...

Chicago Crime Strategy could become a national model. In direct response to the street scene driving the violence,

Chicago's police superintendent, Garry McCarthy, is working with criminologists and other researchers to spearhead a new response that could represent the next major advance in how America polices serious violence.

At its core, the new approach focuses not on crime "hot spots," the traditional target of law enforcement, but on "hot people"—the small number of individuals who account for the vast majority of the crime and murders.[15]

Apostolic intercession causes light to spring forth and new thoughts and ideas that minister justice in every realm and dimension to re-engineer existing structures to come into righteous and just alignment.

Remember, this apostolic sound is light, and as we release the light of eternal truth into the environment of those souls chained in darkness, the light of His love breaks the power of every reasoning and theory that has exalted itself against the knowledge of God.

40 DAYS OF PRAYER IN D.C.

We also had a 40-day prayer assignment in Washington D.C. in 2011. Our assignment was to lay siege to Washington D.C. in the spiritual realm, releasing the light and power of eternal truth in the capital of our nation, thereby dismantling structures of darkness that have governed there according to 2 Cor. 10:4-5.

In order to rally praying people, we built a website, www.dc40.net and announced our intent to lay siege to DC, along with our intent during the pagan high holy days to have intercessors gather in every capital city in our nation and through repentance and prayer, break the demonic power that the Queen of Heaven had been exerting over our nation.

The pagans somehow got wind of it and went ballistic. All over the internet there were pagan blogs addressing the DC40 Prayer War, and confirming everything we had been saying about Columbia being the goddess they worshipped and was the demonic entity ruling the atmosphere over D.C.

We are so grateful to the Lord for exposing the pagans and their strategies to us. Our assignment was to release light into darkness, so He just had them all raise up against us so we could just send the eternal light of His love and truth right into the nest.

One precious witch strongly encouraged them to all download the 51-day prayer guide written by our dear friend Dr. Marlene McMillan and read it into mirrors, in order that they might reverse what we were doing. Bless the Lord! He is great in mercy and His love endures forever. They were reading the eternal word of the Living God that never returns void! We don't care if they read in reverse, right side up or upside down and as you read this chapter stop here for a moment and ask Father for the eternal truth in that word that they read to explode in their hearts this day. We could never have devised such a brilliant strategy!

If you want to learn more about the thunder of apostolic intercession, I strongly recommend that you read Dr. Marlene McMillan's book, *Declaration of Dependence*. It is available at www.whylibertymatters.com/products.php. By the way, I met her through Dr. Bruce Cook ... well, well, well.

Where we spent 40 days of intercession at 1300 Good Hope Road in Washington D.C., a 24/7 House of Prayer has been established and while they were praying, the Lord laid upon their hearts to ask permission to set up a David's Tent of Worship on the Ellipse between the White House and Washington Monument. What they didn't know was that was the very first place that we had prayed on our 40-day assignment one year earlier.

It is always just being obedient to do what Father reveals to you; we are all building on the faithfulness and eternal intercessions of those who have gone before us. So, our obedience to pray and root out, pull down, overthrow and destroy satanic decrees and dedications at the Ellipse has led to the building and planting of 40 days of worship one year later on that strategic site.

You see, I am a product of this kind of apostolic decree. In 1982, I was a drug-addicted drummer and some folks put my name in a tea cup and began to decree that lifestyle was not what I was created for and called me out of darkness into His glorious light. The power of their intercession invaded the darkness and addiction which enslaved me and that light of His love dawned upon me.

No matter how great the darkness, it flees when the light is turned on.

Apostles of God are loosing the lightning of His truth, accompanied by harvesting angels visiting cities throughout the earth; heaven and earth rejoice at the sound of the feast preparing the way of the Lord.

Father in His wisdom has saved for this hour what Chuck Pierce describes as a Triumphant Reserve. This Triumphant Reserve is an apostolic company in every mountain of influence, a company which has gone through the fire of process and are awakening now and beginning to connect and function "as one," advancing the eternal kingdom in the earth. This connecting itself produces a thunder in the realm of the spirit.

The unified sound of the worship released through these apostolic sons releases the terror of the Lord. I heard that sound in Chicago, and as I asked the Lord about the sound of terror that I heard, He said, "What do you think a Living Creature with six wings full of eyes within and without and the head of a lion sounds like when He cries holy?" Believe me, my friends, the enemy is well acquainted with the terror of the Lord.

The gathering clouds produce apostolic thunder.

"Of the increase of His government and of peace there shall be no end, upon the throne of David and over his kingdom, to establish it and to uphold it with justice and with righteousness from the [latter] time forth, even forevermore. The zeal of the Lord of hosts will perform this."
(Isa. 9:7, AMP)

We are privileged to be living in the hour when the anointing and mantles of the eternal march of the Kingdom are converging at the time of the former and latter rain.

While on the same prayer journey in Chicago, I was handed a prophetic word spoken by Maria Woodworth-Etter, who had been scheduled to minister at the Stone Church at the intersection of 37th and Indiana in Chicago for 30 days in July 1913. The glory of the Lord manifested with such a mighty outpouring of healing that her meetings were extended for six months. Near the end of those gatherings, Maria prophesied that what they were experiencing in 1913 was the former rain, but in 100 years, the latter rain would fall.

DECLARATION
OF APOSTOLIC THUNDER

I declare to you the rain is falling now, and that the thunder of the eternal word of the Living God released through the synergy of apostolic voices in the earth, will grow mighty in power as the rain continues to fall and the Ezekiel 47 river continues to rise.

Recently at a gathering of our local ekklesia, we began to sing this apostolic decree: "My words in your mouth are the same as My words in My mouth," says the Lord!

The power of this hour is that these thundering apostles are producing multitudes of apostolic sons who understand governing in the spiritual realm. These sons are invading the mountains of religion, family, education, government, media, arts and entertainment, and business.

The tsunami caused by the earthquake the cross created 2,000 years ago is just now approaching the shoreline.

In our society it seems like light has receded, but the roar of the victory of the blood of the one is now magnified by apostolic sons in every nation!

The angels who fought with Joshua, Gideon, and David have longed as well for this era of apostolic thunder and functioning ekklesia! They are moving in the sound of the thunder as the two camps, the camp of heaven and the camp of earth, move together.

PSALM 29 (AMP)[16]

"Give unto the Lord, O sons of the mighty,
Give unto the Lord glory and strength.

Give to the Lord the glory due to His name;
worship the Lord in the beauty of holiness or in holy array.

The voice of the Lord is upon the waters; the God of glory
thunders; the Lord is upon many (great) waters.

The voice of the Lord is powerful;
the voice of the Lord is full of majesty.

The voice of the Lord breaks the cedars;
yes, the Lord breaks in pieces the cedars of Lebanon.

He makes them also to skip like a calf; Lebanon and Sirion
(Mount Hermon) like a young, wild ox.

The voice of the Lord splits and flashes forth forked lightning.

The voice of the Lord makes the wilderness tremble;
the Lord shakes the Wilderness of Kadesh.

The voice of the Lord makes the hinds bring forth their young,
and His voice strips bare the forests,
while in His temple everyone is saying, Glory!

The Lord sat as King over the deluge;
the Lord [still] sits as King [and] forever!

The Lord will give [unyielding and impenetrable] strength to
His people; the Lord will bless His people with peace."

ENDNOTES

1. http://www.huffingtonpost.com/2012/02/15/chicago-most-corrupt-city_n_1278988.html

2. http://usnews.nbcnews.com/_news/2012/07/26/12972034-nationwide-raids-on-synthetic-drug-labs-lead-to-90-arrests-seizure-of-36-million#.UBG0NvonOgA.email

3. http://abcnews.go.com/Business/high-profile-financial-scandals-months/story?id=17023140#.UC5og5dNuPI.email

4. http://www.chicagotribune.com/news/politics/clout/chi-illinois-house-expels-rep-derrick-smith-over-bribery-charge-20120817,0,4436516.story

5. http://soc.li/WdnGAnX

6. http://articles.chicagotribune.com/2012-06-25/news/chi-study-calls-for-probing-of-political-corruption-in-more-than-60-suburbs--20120625_1_inspector-political-corruption-public-corruption

7. http://abcnews.go.com/Business/comptroller-dixon-illinois-arrested-allegedly-pilfering-30-million/story?id=16164072#.UGwiEfl25wt

8. http://www.cbsnews.com/video/watch/?id=7414574n&tag=pop;videos

9. http://video.foxnews.com/v/1596046196001/occupy-unmasked/?playlist_id=87937

10. http://usnews.nbcnews.com/_news/2012/05/17/11744015-la-suspends-7-cops-for-jump-out-boys-clique?lite

11. http://www.chicagotribune.com/news/sns-rt-us-mexico-drugs-arrest bre84j0b7-20120520,0,4440350.story

12. http://www.huffingtonpost.com/2012/08/07/joaquin-el-chapo-guzman-mexicos-most-wanted_n_1751671.html

13. http://news.yahoo.com/last-colombian-drug-kingpin-falls-crazy-barrera-captured-192433107--abc-news-topstories.html

14. http://www.mysanantonio.com/news/local_news/article/Arrest-could-spur-drug-routes-merger-3899548.php#ixzz28BBrV4gW

15. http://www.chicagomag.com/Chicago-Magazine/The-312/ October-2012/Garry-McCarthys-New-Chicago-Crime-Strategy-Social-Networks-Hot-People/

16. Psalm 29:1 has been called "The Song of the Thunderstorm," a glorious psalm of praise sung during an earthshaking tempest which reminds the psalmist of the time of Noah and the deluge.

ABOUT THE AUTHOR

James Nesbit has an unusual ability to help the Body of Christ see eternal reality through the gift of art. James has worked with many artistic mediums, but in this season works almost exclusively in the digital format.

A portion of his assignment in the earth is a Habakkuk 2 assignment - to write the vision and engrave it so plainly (through digital imagery) that everyone who passes may be able to read it easily and quickly as he hastens by.

It has been said that a picture is worth a thousand words. James believes he, as a prophetic artist, has a responsibility to magnify the words of the prophets, and serves the voice of the prophets by adding sight to sound.

"As we serve one another in preparing the way of the Lord, our gifts accentuate each other, so each joint is joined fitly together supplying the strength the other needs." - James

In 2005 James and his son Isaac (who was 11 years old at the time) worked together for three months creating prophetic art for all 50 U.S. states highlighting the prophetic decrees Dutch Sheets and Chuck Pierce released over each state on the 50 State Tour. James believes strongly that these words are the true prophetic blueprint of America, and created the art so that intercessors throughout the land could have the true vision of their state before their eyes, and with one voice call these United States into the fullness of their prophetic destiny.

Both C. Peter Wagner and Cindy Jacobs have said James is one of the leading prophetic artists in the earth today.

James is also the apostolic overseer of Prepare the Way Ministries. Prepare the Way is a unique, strategic intercessory ministry that deals with "Root Issues" in the heart of America and other nations as the Lord leads.

James was born in the American heartland and the heartland is his assignment; what happens in the heart courses through the veins of America and affects the entirety of this nation from border to border - and the North American continent, for that matter. To learn more about his work or ministry, or to contact James, please visit his websites at www.ptwministries.com or www.jamesnart.com.

CHAPTER TWENTY-SEVEN

UNDERCOVER ASSIGNMENT: APOSTOLIC INTERCESSION TO RESTORE AMERICA

GARY BEATON

I'm about to tell you a very unusual and compelling story, one that you have never heard before. In it I will also share key spiritual principles of "Aligning with the Apostolic" relating to America and its past, present and future.

Any time you align with the true Apostolic, major changes take place in your life. It is in that order that Jesus birthed the Church to function at its highest level. The Apostolic operates outside the four walls of the Church in many forms, as Dr. Cook clearly articulates, because we serve a God who is infinite in all of His ways.

America was birthed by godly men and women appointed to carry the mantle and DNA of the Apostolic in government, politics, law and science. That is why the foundation of this nation has been able to sustain and weather the test of time. The Founders understood the basic precept that men, elected to represent others, through deliberations and agreement, have the power to draft documents to form a Charter. By sealing it with their own signatures, that document and its intent actually has the power to create an entire nation sanctioned under God. That is why the

Declaration of Independence and the U.S. Constitution bear so much weight and authority on earth.

The same holds true with Kings who use a seal or signet ring to carry out royal commands or decrees.

Have you ever considered that the King of Kings may actually have His own Seal or Signet Ring at the Throne of God? The Founders of this nation also understood this Kingly principle and worked together to design America's own two-sided Seal in 1782. Both sides of the seal were not actually seen by the majority of Americans until Franklin Delano Roosevelt had them placed on the back of the one dollar bill in 1935. If we go back to the actual founding Charter of America, it was the Mayflower Compact signed on November 11, 1620 by 41 believers. They were in agreement to claim and settle a land for religious freedom and for God's glory. William Bradford carried the Apostolic mantle for that hour as the leader of that early Plymouth settlement. One true mark of an Apostle is that he will stand unwavering for the truth, regardless of the cost.

Throughout the ensuing years, the U.S. Constitution and the Bill of Rights were ordained to keep this nation intact. Yet, at the founding of America, the enemy had his own designs on this nation, as he does with anything that God desires or ordains. Satan sowed tares and created mixture through the occult in the same foundation, which caused a crack... ever so minute, and beyond the sight of most onlookers. Master Builders will tell you that if there is a crack in the foundation of any structure, over time, it will widen and eventually can cause long-term damage.

I believe that the majority of the Founders were true believers at heart, but clearly some were not. For instance, Ben Franklin was one of our greatest leaders. Truly he will always be one of my personal heroes for his inventiveness, creativity and wisdom. He was gifted beyond measure and is credited for much of what we have in America today through countless agencies and inventions. He served our country in its most pivotal moments of survival as an Ambassador to England and France. We owe much to his genius. He was also one of only six original Founders to sign both the Declaration of Independence and the Constitution. If he were younger during his time in the late 1700's, he certainly would have been considered to be one of our earliest Presidents.

Yet, despite his genius and his countless contributions, there were spiritual issues in his own life that adversely affected the Founding of this nation. He had the anointing and influence of an Apostle, but lacked the conviction of Christ in his heart.

As I stated, many of the most influential Founders were believers, and yet Franklin, by his own admission, was not. Instead, I believe that he blended his beliefs as a deist and his religion of freemasonry. As a printer in Philadelphia in 1730, he printed and distributed the first Masonic Bible in America. He was also elected as the Grand Master of the Pennsylvania Lodge in 1734 and was among those from St. John's Masonic Lodge who laid the cornerstone to the Pennsylvania State Assembly House, which became Independence Hall as we now know it. Sadly, as brilliant as he was, his quest for "Enlightenment" was through the prism of dark light and not the true light of Jesus Christ, Savior of the world.

In the signing of those early documents, God, in his sovereignty, allowed the tares sown at the beginning of America to grow with the wheat. It was just enough to allow the crack to be formed in the foundation and it helped to create an ensuing spiritual battle over the dominion of this nation spanning the next 236 years that would follow. I believe that it was because of this crack, that the Lord placed a call on my life to help bring the needed healing in the spiritual realm to close the gap. In Isaiah 58 we are called to be "...*Repairers of the Breach...*"

CALLED TO THE MINISTRY

I came to the Lord in 1970, just over 40 years ago, with a burning passion to know Him and walk with him as closely as I could. In the late '70s, I was filled with the Spirit and felt a powerful call to ministry. During that time, I was also anointed as a prayer warrior and Intercessor. Despite my feeling "called" to the ministry, the Lord made it very clear to me that He wanted me in television and had purposes for me in the coming years that I wasn't aware of. I just needed to be obedient to His ways and nurture an intimate walk and relationship with Him on a personal level through diligent time in the Word and prayer.

As a veteran in television and broadcast journalism for almost four decades, I've been a documentary producer, director, writer, researcher, historian and editor. The Lord placed me with an apostolic influence in many of the top news and cable outlets in the Media Mountain for many years with a unique purpose and destiny in mind. First, He would use me as a vessel of Light in a dark place, as it's widely understood that the mainstream media is predisposed with a liberal bent. Secondly, the Lord chose to grant me the mantle of an Apostle and Prophet in the spheres of television and media to utilize and release His Kingdom influence on multiple levels.

Beginning in the late '90s, the Lord began waking me up at 2:00 a.m. for prayer. It became my lifestyle to bundle up in the night and spend up to three hours each night in worship and intercession outside under the stars in the country. I was free to sing in the Spirit, play my guitar in worship and also war in prayer. It was the joy of my life to spend that kind of time alone with Him and I've never found anything that compares. I believe it was that foundation of love and intimacy that deepened my relationship and prepared me for my future calling.

At around 5:00 a.m. each morning near the close of my prayer time, I would generally go back inside and take a two-hour nap before I went to my daily job in television. Oftentimes, those would be when I would receive the most remarkable dreams and visions. Prophet Bob Jones once told me that he refers to those early hours as "the time of the trances." I believe it was the Lord's goodness and His way of honoring my love and devotion. He does that for every one of his children in unique ways. This is simply the kindness and love of God.

In November of 1997, I accepted a full-time position as a Senior Producer at Scripps Networks Interactive. On April 18, 2000, I was named Supervising Producer of a new program for HGTV (Home and Garden Television) called "Restore America." On that particular day, there were two dynamic things that struck me. One was that as an Apostolic / Prophetic Intercessor, I was being given an assignment that went beyond the natural realm to position me to somehow make a significant impact spiritually to help "Restore America" through prayer, repentance and intercession.

The second dynamic that struck me was the date itself. I knew because of my knowledge of American History and Longfellow's famous poem, "The Midnight Ride of Paul Revere," that the very day I received the commission to oversee *"Restore America"* was exactly 225 years to the day of Paul Revere's ride! That is what I call a "stunner." How exquisite God is... to confirm a supernatural calling that would reveal the divine intention of "sounding an alarm" of repentance to America through the aid and assistance of a secular company!

It was then that I understood that this was a specific assignment from the Lord, and one that would ultimately launch me into a series of journeys specifically mapped out from heaven like a blueprint to guide me as I traveled America for the next seven years. Each journey would bear its own mark with supernatural confirmations to let me know that I was on track and had "hit the target" in prayer.

In June of 2001, I received a call from a well-seasoned Prophet, Ruth Featherstone, who had seen a vision relating to me and the program *"Restore America."* She called it the "Paneled-Door Vision." In it, she saw a paneled door with an American Flag draped over it. Then she saw a number of famous names, movies and events listed as words in a row from top to bottom on the door. She told me to get a pen so I could write down the names in the exact order in which she saw them. (This is an extremely good example of how the Apostolic and Prophetic can work together in tandem outside the church walls to bring about God's will into the earth). I wrote down all of it exactly as she described it in my journal, even though it didn't have any present-day bearing to me. I had known Ruth for years to be extremely accurate in the prophetic realm and I trusted that it would mean something important along the way. The list began with Mark Twain, Back to the Future, Abraham Lincoln, the Civil War, George Washington, George Bush, etc.

One year later, HGTV (Home and Garden Television) partnered with the National Trust for Historic Preservation and Save America's Treasures, based in Washington, DC, to grant them $1,000,000 a year to parcel between 12 national historic sites needing funding for much-needed restoration. Cooperatively, HGTV and the NTHP worked together to vet and decide on what their first 12 sites would be beginning in late summer of 2002. On May 29th, 2002, I was called to a meeting with HGTV and given the list of the first 12 sites they had selected. I stared at the list in stunned silence because it nearly replicated the list on the paneled-door vision that the Lord had given me through Ruth a year before! Mark Twain's historic home in Hartford, Conn., even topped the list from HGTV exactly as Ruth had seen in her vision. Then Abraham Lincoln's Cottage, with "Back to the Future" in between the two in Ruth's vision.

It was clear that the list HGTV gave me was actually from the Throne Room and the Holy Spirit had supernaturally imparted it through three major secular entities to place in my hands as my first set of prayer and intercessory assignments. As the Supervising Producer for *Restore America*, it would be my responsibility to coordinate the planning and filming of the sites that would air within the series. It was the Father's divine plan to have me produce a high-quality historic television program, while at the same time prophetically work "undercover" to discover what was out of sync in history that needed redeeming.

The "Back to the Future" principle for believers is that by repairing the past through repentance of sin, Time can ripple forward and the future can turn out to be the way the

Lord desires and intended it to be. In Dan. 2:21-22 it says, *"He changes the times and the seasons; He removes kings and sets up kings. He gives wisdom to the wise and knowledge to those who have understanding! He reveals the deep and secret things; He knows what is in the darkness, and the light dwells with Him"* (AMP, author's emphasis).

STANDING IN THE GAP

The key to mending the breach is standing in the gap as it is described in Ezek. 22:30: *"And I sought a man among them who should build up the wall and stand in the gap before Me for the land, that I should not destroy it, but I found none"* (AMP, author's emphasis).

The Lord was always faithful to confirm the mending of Time with signs and wonders to assure me that I was on track. It was a profound journey that would ultimately have me travel to countless locations across America. Through those years all was accomplished with precision because I was supported by a remarkable team of prophetic intercessors who helped to hold up my arms and enable me to fulfill my missions. In that way it was always a team effort and it was God's way of providing alignment and covering through my local church.

The Lord had taken me to Philadelphia many times, but one journey stands out more than the others to confirm my point about healing the crack in the foundation of American history. After completing my normal shoot for the *Restore America* program on a Friday afternoon in April of 2004, I was invited to dinner with the Tourism leadership of the city. During the course of dinner, the topic of history shifted to William Penn and the founding of Pennsylvania with Penn's famous "Charter of Privileges" in 1701.

Prior to 1701, King Charles II of England owed William Penn's father, Admiral Sir William Penn, a vast sum of money from a loan. After Admiral Penn's passing, on March 4, 1681, the King gave William Penn the tract of land we now know as Pennsylvania in return for the debt. William held to such strong Quaker beliefs, that he wanted Pennsylvania to become a haven for anyone seeking religious freedom. The principles that Penn set forth in the "Charter of Privileges" eventually became one of the primary guiding influences for the U.S. Constitution.

It was also during that dinner with the Philadelphia Tourism Department, where I learned that in 1751, the Pennsylvania Assembly decided to honor the 50-year Jubilee, by ordering a Bell that would hang in the Pennsylvania State House steeple. It ultimately became known as "The Liberty Bell." As we spoke of these things, the Tourism Director asked if I would like to have a special viewing of the Liberty Bell and Independence Hall the following morning. I knew this could have only opened up because of my position with *Restore America*, by the hand of God and for a divine purpose, so I agreed wholeheartedly.

The next day, Saturday, April 24, I drove into the Old City of Philadelphia before dawn, prior to the day's events. I was scheduled to meet with the Director of Special Events with the National Park Service at 10:00 a.m. My role with "*Restore America*" had opened a miraculous door of favor to be granted a private tour of such a historic site before the day's public tours began.

A little after 6:00 a.m., I parked the car near Independence Hall on 5th and Chestnut, directly in front of the American Philosophical Society, which happened to have been created by Benjamin Franklin in 1743. It was a cool, brisk autumn morning and very few people were out on the streets.

I was four hours ahead of time, but I sensed an urgency that this day of prayer was an important one that would cause a powerful shift for the nation's destiny. I sat in my car and called my intercessor friend, Ruth, to join with me to pray and agree for God's will. As we were praying, Ruth felt that the Lord was clearly saying that He was going to the core of the Founding of America that day, and that I was to specifically call for a Kingdom alignment regarding the documents that were signed in Independence Hall. We asked that the Lord guide my day, lead me to where I needed to be and have me pray all that He wanted me to pray along the way.

I began to ask that the Holy Spirit go to the very core of this nation and that He would bring the critical alignment He desired and "loose" the Blood of Jesus to the roots of Philadelphia and to the roots at the founding of America.

In Matt. 18:18 Jesus said, *"Whatsoever ye shall bind on earth shall be bound in heaven: and whatsoever ye shall loose on earth shall be loosed in heaven"* (KJV, author's emphasis). For years, we have bound the powers of darkness, but rarely had I ever loosed anything in prayer except for someone held captive by darkness. It was through this set of historical journeys that the Lord taught me the principle of "loosing the Blood" in warfare against the adversary.

Just before 7:00 a.m., as I was vocally and fervently, "loosing the Blood of the Lamb" to the roots of this nation and the American government formed at Independence Hall, only one block away, I began to hear the sound of sirens behind me. I looked in my rear-view mirror, and to my shock, there were a number of fire engines coming past Independence

Hall toward me on Chestnut Street. A fire Chief leading the procession in a smaller red vehicle pulled directly in front of my car and jumped out. He started banging feverishly on my windshield and yelling for me to "get out"! In total surprise, I jumped out of my car, but he told me instead that he wanted me to move my car out of there. He went on to tell me that a fire had started under the street, directly beneath my car in front of Benjamin Franklin's "American Philosophical Society"!

In total amazement, I jumped back into my car and drove a few blocks away and parked. As I quickly made my way back to the scene, a total of four fire engines had pulled up and surrounded the area. The first was Number 8 (New Beginnings). I sensed immediately that the fire under my car was a direct result of the prayer to miraculously confirm the power of the Blood released to the "roots" of history in the Spirit. The Lord wanted me to know that there is a distinct correlation between the natural realm and the supernatural when power is released through prayer.

The firemen put the fire out and there was little damage. They were all completely puzzled at how it could have begun. Fire, in terms of the scriptures, is not always destructive, as seen in Exodus with the Burning Bush and the Pillar of Fire. In the 2nd Chapter of Acts it was also seen on the day of Pentecost where fire appeared as cloven tongues upon the believers' heads.

Fire often cauterizes wounds and I believe that the Lord used this as an example to confirm that He was answering the prayer immediately to help seal up the crack and heal the wounds from centuries before. That was just the beginning of my day, but my, what a way to get things started! It was also faith-building since the Word says that *"The effectual fervent prayer of a righteous man availeth much"* (KJV, author's emphasis). We are all righteous before God because of the sacrifice of His Son, but He wants to encourage us that the dynamic of "loosing the Blood" releases tremendous power in prayer. I have experienced many supernatural events before, but that event will always stand out as remarkable and it greatly increases my awe of Him.

APPLY THE BLOOD

I believe as the Lord's return approaches, one of the greatest strategies from Heaven for the equipping of the Church will be an overwhelming emphasis on the power and effectiveness of the Blood for protection and spiritual warfare. In Rev. 12:11 it says *"And they overcame (conquered) him by means of the blood of the Lamb and by the utterance of their testimony, for they did not love and cling to life even when faced with death"* (AMP, author's emphasis).

As the firemen did their work to put out the fire and restore the area to peace, I felt to go across the street to "Founders Park" as a place of serenity for prayer. It's a beautiful setting with park benches surrounded by hedges and flowers. At the center of the park is a bronze statue of a young man holding up to the sky what appears to be the rolled up scrolls of the Declaration and Constitution. I was totally alone and felt the presence of the Lord to pray and repent with Communion for the Founders who had deliberate sin in their lives and anything else the enemy used to sow tares in the founding of America.

In that time of repentance and tears, I applied the Blood to the fracture in Time to heal the breach and called for the restoration of America, so she might finish her course and complete the task she was created for. I did this in public as I often do and as inconspicuously as possible. At one point I looked up from my papers to see if anyone else had entered the park. I was surprised to see a woman dressed in a full-length flowing white gown standing motionless at the entrance of the park. She was actually staring at me. I wasn't sure what to think of her at first because it seemed unusual for her to be wearing such a beautiful gown so early on a Saturday morning. I glanced back down at my papers momentarily and then looked back up at her and in no more than a second or two she had instantly vanished!

There was a waist-high-iron fence that encircled the park, so it would have been impossible for her to make it down the sidewalk in either direction without being seen...even if she had been running. I believe that clearly, she was an Angel who had appeared momentarily as a messenger from the Throne to confirm my assignment and convey the Lord's satisfaction that I was repenting with Communion to help bring Apostolic re-alignment for America's destiny.

At 10:00 a.m., I met the NPS Ranger at the National Park Mall where the Liberty Bell is now on display. He greeted me warmly and then took me to the Liberty Bell and began explaining its history. I understood from the dinner conversation the evening before how the bell arrived in 1752 and that it cracked with its first ringing. The Ranger went on to tell me the rest of the story. The Bell was then melted down and re-cast because the composition of metals used to create the Bell needed adjusting. Once it had been re-cast and hung in the tower for the second time, it cracked again upon ringing! It created such a paradox within the State of Pennsylvania that some considered sending it back to England. But instead, they decided to hire John Pass and John Stow to melt it down a third time and re-cast it with the famous verse from Lev. 25:10 *"... **Proclaim LIBERTY throughout all the Land to all the Inhabitants thereof...**"* (KJV).

It was in that moment of the Ranger's story that it hit me like a lightning bolt. The crack in the Liberty Bell was a prophetic picture in the natural of the very crack in the spiritual foundation of the nation! No wonder it cracked every time they re-cast it, even with the scriptural reference on it. God wanted to reveal one of the mysteries of the ages in terms of its famous crack and the "mixture" in the Bell's composition...confirming again the mixture in the composition of America's founding.

After our visit to the Liberty Bell, we crossed the street to Independence Hall. The Ranger took me through each room of Pennsylvania's original State House and carefully explained its role in history. When we entered the room where the Founders met as the Continental Congress, I felt an almost reverential hush while standing where such profound history was made by men of resolute courage.

I felt honored to be in that place and we lingered there a while to take in the moment, surrounded by the echoes of living history.

We then proceeded to the second floor and the Ranger asked me if I would like to go up into the Bell and Clock tower. I could hardly believe my ears since I knew that it wasn't accessible to the public. But again, only God's favor could open such a special door. The Ranger said that the last group he had taken up into the tower was Senator Ted Kennedy and his family, shortly before he passed away.

As we ascended the winding wooden staircase, we were surrounded by the original massive framing timbers. Each step I took felt surreal. We were climbing up the very tower from which the Liberty Bell's peal had proclaimed America's independence and the birth of a new nation in 1776. This was a defining moment.

When we reached the top of the platform, the Ranger turned to me and asked if I knew that someone had just finished filming a movie here? I was surprised and asked what it was. He said, "It's called *National Treasure* and it has to do with the Founding Fathers and a secret treasure map that Benjamin Franklin, a Freemason, had placed in invisible ink on the back of the Declaration of Independence. They were here shooting it, right where you are standing, just a few months ago." The movie came out later that same year.

The Lord is truly amazing in His ability to reveal and confirm His ways when we walk with Him in intimacy. Only God in His infinite majesty could weave such an incredible plan of redemption. The real treasure is the Lord's unique ability to use the Apostolic to re-align this nation for His purposes, when His people are in tune with His heart and are like the men of Issachar, "who understood the times and knew what to do."

This was one of more than a dozen strategic apostolic intercession assignments the Lord has given me through the years in my role as a media producer, and in conjunction with my work on this series and others. I will save the full story of these other assignments for my own book, which is in process. What assignments has the Lord given you lately? And what have you done with them?

ABOUT THE AUTHOR

Gary Beaton is an ardent believer with a heart to see the glory of God revealed in the lives of believers everywhere. He's had an intimate walk with the Lord for four decades and a power-filled and prophetic intercessory life with Christ. His burning passion is for the harvest and to see lives miraculously healed, restored and transformed. Gary speaks and ministers with the goal of revealing the majesty of God through a focus on the Blood of Christ. His heart is to encourage believers to see the supernatural manifested as part of their daily lives and to experience a passionate joy in their walk with the Lord.

Gary's career, spanning nearly 40 years, has been in Television as a Producer and as an award-winning Broadcast Journalist. As a Producer, Director, Writer and Editor, his production credits include ABC News *20/20, Nightline, Good Morning America, World News Tonight* with Peter Jennings and *This Week with David Brinkley*. He has also traveled extensively worldwide in the news industry, producing for PBS' *MacNeil/Lehrer News Hour, USA Today* and Swiss, French, German and Italian television. Gary has also been awarded 12 National Telly Awards for his outstanding work in documentaries and his contributions in the field of Broadcast Journalism.

For more information or to contact Gary you can reach him at www.transformationglory.com or visit his video posted on YouTube at http://youtu.be/2p6uCkRAOjM. This video was posted Sept. 17, 2012, on the Feast of Trumpets, exactly 225 years from the date of the signing of the U.S. Constitution in 1787.

CHAPTER TWENTY-EIGHT

PRAYING LIKE THE APOSTLES

BOB CATHERS

Apostles were established with the resurrection of Christ; they embodied a new office in the church. Jesus himself was an apostle, according to Heb. 3:1, *"Therefore, holy brothers and sisters, who share in the heavenly calling, fix your thoughts on Jesus, whom we acknowledge as our apostle and high priest."*

Clearly, the ministry of the Apostle was chief in establishing the church of the Lord Jesus Christ. And the office of Apostle is still vital, as the Lord uses it to this day, to establish His church.

HOW TO PRAY: SEEKING GOD FIRST

Based on Luke's historical account, Jesus' men asked Him, *"Lord, teach us to pray"* (Luke 11:1). Jesus responded with what is now known as "The Lord's Prayer." (See also Matt. 6:9-13.)

According to Matthew (who travelled with Jesus), "The Lord's Prayer" derived from Jesus' Sermon on the Mount.

But before He imparted "The Lord's Prayer," Jesus warned against vain repetitions (Matt. 6:7-8).

> "But when you pray, do not use vain repetitions as the heathen do. For they think that they will be heard for their many words. Therefore do not be like them. For your Father knows the things you have need of before you ask Him."
> (Matt. 6:7-8)

Jesus began "The Lord's Prayer" by saying, "In this manner, therefore, pray." He then laid out the foundational principles of prayer:

- To approach our Father with sonship (or as equally, as daughters)
- With praise
- Calling forth earth to be like the kingdom of heaven
- Asking for daily bread (Word or revelation)
- Thanking Him for His forgiving nature toward us
- Refusing to hold seeds of unforgiveness against others
- Thanking Him for freedom from temptation or lusts
- Deliverance from the enemy's plans
- Glorifying God for his eternal power

Jesus was not reciting a rote, 10-second prayer. There are other Apostolic prayers beyond this, but Jesus, the Chief Apostle, instructed us to look here first.

KNOWING GOD:
THE PRAYER OF JESUS

Jesus gave us a major revelation about prayer: it is an intimate relationship between man and God. Prayer is truly about knowing God. It is not about asking God for what we need. (There is a time to pray for needs, discussed later.)

Paul confirmed this in Eph. 1:18-19, by praying that we would come to know God.

> *"That the God of our Lord Jesus Christ, the Father of glory,*
> *may give to you the spirit of wisdom and revelation in the*
> *knowledge of Him, the eyes of your understanding being*
> *enlightened, that you may know what is the hope of His*
> *calling, what are the riches of the glory of*
> *His inheritance in the saints."*
> (Eph. 1:18-19)

Most people think prayer is about asking God for what they need, and this mindset is the reason that so many prayers are not answered.

Matt. 6:8 says, *"Therefore do not be like the heathen. For your Father knows the things you have need of before you ask Him."*

If we continually ask God for things of this world (mammon) we are praying as a heathen. Matt. 6:24 explains why this presents an internal conflict:

> *"You cannot serve both God and mammon."*
> (Matt. 6:24)

Yet many of our prayers attempt to turn God into the God of mammon.

In Matt. 6:33, Jesus told us that if we seek first His kingdom and His righteousness, He will add everything unto us that the Gentiles seek. It is not that God is against your being prosperous - He is not. It is about praying in God's order and seeking Him first.

> *"But seek first the kingdom of God and His righteousness, and all these things shall be added unto you."*
> (Matt. 6:33)

(handwritten: favorite scripture)

HIS RIGHTEOUSNESS

Note the word "righteousness," or rightstanding with God. This is an essential element of relational prayer. To truly have a relationship with our heavenly Father, we must believe He loves us as we are, because He created us to be who we are. We must shed our sin consciousness and the condemnation that it carries. We must dare to believe the scriptures that tell us that we are kings and priests unto God (Rev. 1:6), joint heirs with Christ (Rom. 8:17) and seated with Christ in heavenly places (Eph. 2:6).

> *"Just as He chose us in Him before the foundation of the world, that we should be holy and without blame before Him in love."*
> (Eph. 1:4)

> *"What is the exceeding greatness of His power toward us who believe, according to the working of His mighty power, which He worked in Christ when He raised Him from the dead and seated Him at the His right hand in the heavenly places, far above all principality and power and might and*

*dominion, and every name that is named, not only in this
age but also that which is to come."*
(Eph. 1:19-21)

*"Whoever does not practice righteousness is not of God, nor
is he who does not love his brother."*
(1 John 1:10)

Moreover, through righteousness, we can have the faith of empowerment, as Jesus said that those who believe on His name shall cast out demons, heal the sick, etc. (Mark 16:17-18).

*"And the glory which You gave Me, I have given them, that
they may be one just as We are one."*
(John 17:22)

*"Most assuredly, I say to you, he who believes in Me, the
works that I do, he will do also, and greater works than these
he will do, because I go to My Father."*
(John 14:12)

INTIMATE RELATIONSHIP WITH GOD

*"Pray therefore like this: Our Father who is in heaven,
hallowed be Your name."*
(Matt. 6:9)

Jesus changed the way we pray from "Almighty God" to "Father," shifting it to a personal, loving, caring relationship. All prayer should begin with us just reconnecting with our heavenly Father, coming into His presence and being with Him.

Many years ago, I was praying and seeking God. I had been praying in tongues for four hours, when I heard God tell me that He wanted to give me a new house. I already had a house that I was quite happy with, but since God was offering this gift, I told God what I would desire:

1. Location on a cul-de-sac
2. Tennis Court, so my wife and I could play tennis together
3. Pool, as it gets hot in Southern California
4. Spa, to relax my muscles after working out

That is the house that we live in today. We got that house without selling our original home, and we did not have to pay a dime to do it. Seek first His kingdom!

EPHESIANS 6:
WARFARE

We also pray for God's kingdom to manifest on earth as it is in heaven. Matt. 12:25 reveals that there are two opposing, divided kingdoms: God's and satan's. So, when we pray for God's kingdom to come, we enter into that war. For one kingdom to occupy, the other must be displaced. That alone is a revelation, and at times, it can be a battle just to start to pray – and sometimes the prayer itself can be a battle.

"In conclusion, be strong in the Lord; draw your strength from Him. Put on God's whole armor, that you may be able to stand up against all the strategies and the deceits of the devil. For we wrestle not against flesh and blood, but against the powers, against the world rulers of this present darkness, against spirit forces of wickedness in the heavenly sphere.

*Therefore put on God's armor, that you may be able to resist
and stand your ground on the evil day, and having done all,
to stand. Stand therefore, having tightened the belt of truth
around your loins, and having put on the breastplate of
integrity and of right standing with God. And having shod
your feet in preparation of the Gospel of peace. Lift up over all
the shield of faith, upon which you can quench all the flaming
missiles of the wicked one. And take the helmet of salvation
and the sword of the Spirit, which is the word of God. Pray at
all times in the Spirit with all prayer. To that end, keep alert
and watch the strong purpose and perseverance, interceding
in behalf of all the saints."*
(Eph. 6:10-18)

The armor we wear is prayer armor, whereby we
battle the thoughts and mindsets that satan tries to release
on this earth. Satan's foundation is the love of money (or the
lust of a thing). But, to bring forth God's kingdom, we must
first understand what His foundations are.

GOD'S FOUNDATIONS: LOVE, LIFE AND LIGHT

God is:

1. Love
2. Life
3. Light

Following are several key Scriptures addressing each of
these attributes of God.

LOVE

*"God is love, and he who abides in love abides in God,
and God in him."*
(1 John 4:16)

*"If anyone loves me, he will keep My word; and My Father
will love him, and We will come to him and make
Our home with him."*
(John 14:23)

*"For God so loved the world, that He gave His only begotten
Son, that whoever believes in Him, should not perish,
but have everlasting life."*
(John 3:16)

*"A new commandment I give you: that you love one another
as I have loved you, that you also love one another.
By this all will know that you are my disciples,
if you have love for one another."*
(John 13:34-35)

LIFE

*"I am the way, the truth and the life.
No one comes to the Father except through Me."*
(John 14:6)

"I am the bread of life."
(John 6:48)

*"I have come that they may have life,
and that they may have it more abundantly."*
(John 10:10)

"Concerning the Word of life – the life was manifested."
(1 John 1:1-2)

"The words that I speak to you are spirit, and they are life."
(John 6:63)

LIGHT

"God is light, and in Him is no darkness at all."
(1 John 1:1-5)

*"I am the light of the world. He who follows me shall not walk
in darkness, but have the light of life."*
(John 8:12)

*"That was the true Light which gives light to
every man who comes into the world."*
(John 1:9)

*"In Him was life, and the life that was the light of men.
And the light shines in the darkness, and the darkness
did not comprehend it."*
(John 1:4-5)

*"The darkness is passing away, and the true light is already
shining. He who says he is in the light, and hates his brother,
is in darkness until now."*
(1 John 1:8-10)

When we pray with kingdom mindsets, we pray for Light, which is revelation. Love is healed relationships. And Life is healing, miracles and blessing. These are all things that Paul prayed for in his writings.

1. Light: Eph. 1:17: Paul prays for a spirit of wisdom and revelation in the knowledge of God.

2. Life: Eph. 1:14: Paul also prayed that we know the greatness of God's power.

3. Love: Eph. 3:17-19: Paul prayed that we know every aspect of His love, which surpasses human knowledge.

Paul's primary prayers were:

1. Eph. 1:15-23

2. Eph. 3:14-21

3. Col. 1:9-14

Through these three prayers, we understand how the great apostle Paul prayed, and what his objectives in prayer were. By praying in alignment with God's will and purposes, God will ultimately take care of our needs. Consider some of Paul's main objectives in prayer, in Eph. 1:17 and Col. 1:9-10.

"I keep asking that the God of our Lord Jesus Christ, the glorious Father, may give you the Spirit of wisdom and revelation, so that you may know Him better."
(Eph. 1:17)

"For this reason, since the day we heard about you, we have not stopped praying for you. We continually ask God to fill you with the knowledge of His will through all the wisdom and understanding that the Spirit gives, so that you may live a life worthy of the Lord and please Him in every way:

bearing fruit in every good work, growing
in the knowledge of God."
(Col. 1:9-10)

SATAN'S KINGDOM: LUST

"For the love of money is a root of all evils; it is through this
craving that some have been led astray and have wandered
from the faith and pierced themselves
through with many pangs."
(1 Tim. 6:10)

The love of money or the lust of a thing is the root or foundation of all evil. It is satan's foundation. It is how he operates his kingdom.

1. Satan said he would exalt his throne above the throne of God. He lusted for what he did not have.

2. Satan deceived Eve in the Garden into believing that she needed something that she did not (to become more like God), thus causing her to lust for it.

3. Satan used lust on Judas, who betrayed Christ for 30 pieces of silver. The foundation had previously been laid there, as Judas was already stealing from the offering plate.

4. The Holy Spirit took the lives of Ananias and Sapphira because they nearly brought the foundation of lust (by lying about fully divesting their property) to the early church.

5. Jesus was offered all the kingdoms of the world (a lust for power) if only He would worship satan.

Lust is satan's foundation, and how he builds his kingdom. This was the last revelation he had before he was cast down from heaven, and he still works by it today.

So, we cannot build a foundation of prayer on needs and lusts. Jesus demonstrated this, when He declared that His house would be a house of prayer in Matt. 21:12-15 by cleansing the temple and the money changers.

"Jesus entered the temple courts and drove out all who were buying and selling there. He overturned the tables of the money changers and the benches of those selling doves. 'It is written,' He said to them, 'My house will be called a house of prayer,' but you are making it 'a den of robbers.' The blind and the lame came to him at the temple, and He healed them. But when the chief priests and the teachers of the law saw the wonderful things He did and the children shouting in the temple courts, 'Hosanna to the Son of David,' they were indignant."
(Matt. 21:12-15)

KNOWING GOD:
THE PRAYERS OF PAUL

Praying to know God, His heart, His desires and who He really is, was a major objective of Paul when he prayed. According to Ps. 10:3-7, Moses knew God's ways, as did Abraham. And Jas. 2:23 indicates that one person who knows God can do more in prayer than three million who don't (Moses vs. Israel). It should be our daily goal and the cry of our hearts to know God better, and to know God's call and inheritance. Our loving Father wants to be known, even as we are known.

Consider also Eph. 1:18 and Col. 1:12:

"I pray that the eyes of your heart may be enlightened in order that you may know the hope to which He has called you, the riches of His glorious inheritance in His holy people."
(Eph. 1:18)

"Giving joyful thanks to the Father, who has qualified you to share in the inheritance of His holy people in the kingdom of light."
(Col. 1:12)

KNOW THE CALL OF GOD

We need to know the call of God and the inheritance He has given to us. Many Christians beg God for things He has already given to us, through His promises. Instead of continually praying for things we already have or need, we need to pray to know who we are and what we have.

Understand God's power in us, and our authority over demon power.

Meditate on Eph. 1:19-21, Eph. 3:16-20 and Col. 1:11-13.

"And his incomparably great power for us who believe. That power is the same as the mighty strength He exerted when He raised Christ from the dead and seated Him at His right hand in the heavenly realms, far above all rule and authority, power and dominion, and every name that is invoked, not only in the present age but also in the one to come."
(Eph. 1:19-21)

*"I pray that out of His glorious riches He may strengthen
you with power through His Spirit in your inner being, so
that Christ may dwell in your hearts through faith. And I
pray that you, being rooted and established in love, now to
Him who is able to do immeasurably more than all we ask or
imagine, according to His power that is at work within us."*
(Eph. 3:16-17, 20)

*"Being strengthened with all power according to His glorious
might so that you may have great endurance and patience.
For He has rescued us from the dominion of darkness and
brought us into the kingdom of the Son He loves."*
(Col. 1:11, 13)

In Matt. 16:18, Jesus said the gates of hell will not prevail
against His church. Jesus also said the first sign we would
manifest as a believer is to cast out devils (Mark 16:17) and
that the armor we wear in prayer protects us against the
attacks of demonic spirits (Eph. 6:10-18). That is why we
need to pray – to understand the power and authority that
God has given us.

To be effective in prayer, we should have encounters with
demonic spirits. Paul himself was buffeted by an unclean
spirit and cried out to God for deliverance, but God told
him he already had enough grace to win that battle.

God never stripped man of his original authority that God
gave him in the Garden (Gen. 1:26). David confirmed that
man still retained that same authority (Ps. 8:3-9). We still
have that same authority today. And Jesus reconfirmed it in
Mark 11:23. When He said, *"Whoever says to this mountain,
be removed and cast into the sea,"* He meant both heathen and
believers.

"Truly I tell you, if anyone says to this mountain, 'Go, throw
yourself into the sea,' and does not doubt in their heart but
believes that what they say will happen,
it will be done for them."
(Mark 11:23)

Under New Testament grace, our authority is even greater. Paul said that we can come boldly to the throne of grace (Heb. 4:16).

"Let us then approach God's throne of grace with confidence,
so that we may receive mercy and find grace to help us in our
time of need."
(Heb. 4:16)

Boldness equates to authority. Jesus exhorted the church to both pray and command with our God-given authority.

PRAY TO KNOW GOD'S LOVE

"So that Christ may dwell in your hearts through faith. And I
pray that you, being rooted and established in love, may have
power, together with all the Lord's holy people, to grasp how
wide and long and high and deep is the love of Christ, and to
know this love that surpasses knowledge - that you may be
filled to the measure of all the fullness of God."
(Eph. 3:17-19)

God is love: that says it all! We cannot ignore the most important aspect of God's Kingdom — His nature. God's kingdom is built on love, God's word is love, and love is the key foundation we need to pray into our lives.

Satan's kingdom is fear, hate, deception, death, destruction, theft and pride. Many people are confused and think these things are strong and authoritative, but love is the greatest power in the universe. In Gal. 5, Paul said faith works by love. But the enemy of our soul wants us to focus on needs and wants, instead of God's foundation.

God's Foundation = pure Love

Satan's Foundation = the love or Lust of money or other worldly things

APOSTOLIC, REVELATORY PRAYER

I invite you to pray this prayer with me now:

"My father in heaven, I come boldly to your throne of grace in the name of your Son and my Savior the Lord Jesus Christ of Nazareth. I ask in His name that You give unto me the spirit of wisdom and revelation in my knowledge of You, and that I am filled with the knowledge of Your will in all wisdom and spiritual understanding, increasing in my knowledge of You, Father.

"And I pray Father that the eyes of my heart are enlightened, so that I know the hope to which You have called me, and the riches of the glorious inheritance You have given me. Father, show me the immeasurable greatness of Your power, according to the working of Your mighty power which you worked in Christ when You raised Him from the dead and seated Him at Your own right hand in heavenly places, far above all principality, power, might and dominion and every name that is named — not only in this world, but also in that which is to come.

"Father, I pray that You pour out Your great grace upon me as You strengthen me with might by Your Spirit in my inner man, that Christ dwells in my heart by faith, and that I am rooted and grounded in love. Help me, Father, to comprehend with all Saints what is the breadth, length, depth, and height and to know the love of Christ, which passes knowledge, that I am filled with all the fullness of God. I pray in faith and believe that I receive these things. Thank you, Heavenly Father. Amen."

PRAYING IN TONGUES

No discussion of Apostolic prayer and Paul's prayers is complete without an exhortation to speak in the Holy Ghost, in unknown tongues. Paul said that he spoke in tongues more than anyone. Of all the ways that I pray, praying in tongues affects me the most, empowers me the most, strengthens me and brings me continual revelation. John G. Lake, one of the great healing ministries of all times, said that prayer in the Spirit was the making of his ministry.

> *"But you, beloved, building yourselves up on your*
> *most holy faith, praying in the Holy Spirit."*
> (Jude 20)

Our faith is in Jesus Christ. The way to build that Faith is by praying in the Holy Spirit. The job of the Holy Spirit is to reveal Christ to our heart and mind. If we desire to know the voice of God, that is the fastest, safest way to do so.

This short, introductory chapter on this topic is only meant to serve as an overview of various types of prayer. Seek God daily, and ask the Holy Spirit to show you how to pray.

Jesus said, *"My house shall be called a house of prayer."* (Matt. 21:13). Truly, God will bless us, His church, when we make His foundations our foundations in prayer.

ABOUT THE AUTHOR

Dr. Bob Cathers was born in Belfast, Northern Ireland, and immigrated with his family to the United States at age 4 and was raised in Sylmar, Calif. At age 20, Bob attended Rhema Bible Training Center in Oklahoma and while there, God gave him a vision regarding Heb. 1:8. From this verse came the acronym, SOARING, the Scepter of Authority and Righteousness in God.

At age 23, Dr. Cathers established his first church, which he pastored for 20 years. At the same time, he also established other churches and ministries, which included a Bible school. After he received a word from God, Dr. Cathers began a new work, which was to establish a Gathering Place learning center, over which he is the Apostle. The Gathering Place was established as a prototype of a new kind of church based on the righteousness of God and the right-standing of believers before Him.

In November 2006, Dr. Cathers was presented with an honorary doctorate by the Latin University of Theology, which has been a major catalyst for new opportunities for him to minister both inside and outside of the church. Recently, Dr. Cathers has been ministering to high authorities within the governments of Uganda, Kenya, and Burundi, in East Africa. He has also been hosting financial seminars for local businessmen in these countries as well. Locally, he has been teaching Righteousness Revolution and Paramount seminars in various locations and cities. Dr. Bob is continually expanding his Church, The Gathering Place, as a learning center. To learn more or contact him, visit his websites www.thegatheringsimi.com and www.robertcathers.com.

CHAPTER TWENTY-NINE

APOSTLES TO THE BOARDROOM

DR. STAN JEFFERY

The Boardroom Prophet is a director or chairman that has God's anointing and is charged to direct and speak to each other and into their companies with the wisdom, ways, and strategies that He provides. Boardroom Prophets is an organization that was started in 2006 with a group of Christian business owners and directors who could see the need for support in the boardroom (from sole directors to corporate boards) for directors and chairpersons. It is part of Christ in Business (CiB) Group that has been set up to bring support to the body of Christ as it functions in business, but predominantly the business owners.

It started with words and guidance to reclaim Sydney. During this time, I was the Director of the University of Ballarat Technology Park in Victoria, Australia. With my wife Jane, we had one week a month in Sydney when we travelled about 1000 Km on Saturday and went back to Ballarat the following Sunday. At that time, we were looking to establish a Christian business incubator at the facility in Christian City Church in Silverwater, a suburb of Sydney, and visited the church there twice a month.

CLAIMING THE CITY FOR GOD

During this time, I had a word from God in September, 2004, during the morning message. While the pastor was speaking, there was a picture of Sydney displayed on the projector screen at the front of the church and I was looking at the picture of Sydney when I felt a strong direction from God to help take Sydney for Jesus and His body.

This was not in the normal way people think, but to actually own it in the body of Christ. This is because the possessions of the unjust are placed in store for the just. I believe the time is right to claim them back for Christ.

THE HARD WORD FROM GOD

The next stage of the word came the next weekend when I believed that God said that He wanted me to lead it and organize the teams. This was not what I wanted to hear. It was okay when someone else was to do it, but now I had the unenviable task.

I felt we should go to the central business district, map it out, and claim a building each (one person or group to a building), praying it into the kingdom of God.

This, I believed, meant to find out who owns it. (At this stage, I naively thought that people owned the buildings).

- If they are Christian owners, meet with them and explain the vision.

- If they are not, then pray them into the kingdom.

- Or claim the building and prepare to buy it, if God leads us to.

I believe God wanted the majority of the Sydney CBD owned by Christians soon.

THE PRESSURE WAS ON FROM GOD

I didn't actually know how to go about this and, as a result, about two years later in April, 2006, God reminded me again at Balls Head Reserve near North Sydney. God led me to go to Balls Head Reserve overlooking the City of Sydney, where I prayed, seeking the name of the controlling sprit over the city and believed it was called, "Greed and Avarice."

God said that He owns the city even now, that Satan had stolen it and God was claiming it back. He said that I must start with the tallest building first and that Jane, the family, and I need to start and develop the process. I asked how to find the tallest building, as the land was undulating, and then God indicated that I should take a photograph and work on the one that was highest from that.

Then, on Easter Sunday in 2006 in my journaling, God said to me, "Yes, tomorrow, I want you to go to the city and start the plan I have given you. Find the tallest building, walk around it, find out its name and the owners, and pray each day for them to come to me and I will receive some and some will not come. Do not worry; I am in control. Do this and I will bless you."

On Easter Monday, I went to Sydney and found the tallest building was Governor Phillips tower and the Governor Macquarie tower at 1 Farrer Place. I sensed a spirit of control was over the building.

On the way back to Ballarat the next day, I felt God was telling me the plan.

- To find the name of the owners, and if they are not an individual, then find the company.

- Seek the chairman and the directors, plus the CEO. Pray for them each day by name.

- When the time is right, seek a word from God to send to their board meeting.

- Then seek to meet with the board.

- Then seek out who the Christians are and pray with them.

In my journal for May, 2006, God said, "Yes, I am leading you and guiding you. Do you not think that I cannot bring someone alongside to help? Yes, I can. Do you not think I can resource my plan? Yes, I can. Yes, I have all in hand. All I need you to do is to move forward in the direction and with the plan I have given you to do. Do it, because I have not asked you because you know how or when it will happen. Yes, do it for me. I will bring everything into order as you do this. Yes, I want Sydney to belong to my Son and His body, which you are part of. Do this and I will return to my people all that has been stolen from them."

Later in May, 2006, at my church while the pastor was ministering, I saw something like a fountain with God's blessing flowing mostly into dry, cracked ground. I felt the need for the fountain to be flowing out of the tallest building over the city and the need to look at the building next to the current one where the blessings will flow into.

All didn't happen as I expected, but this was the start of the long road that we have been on to grow and work with directors and chairmen. The first letters were sent out soon after this second prompting by God.

SYDNEY BUILDING OWNERS

In 2007, I believe God told me that He also wanted to run and own the companies in Australia. This included those that owned Sydney and influenced its operation and directions. He had me send letters to the three chairmen of the listed companies that owned the tallest building and the one next to it in Sydney city, as mentioned before. I had a response from the three chairmen—one of them, let's call him "Chairman John," was positive (although NonChristian) and I have been meeting with him for the last five years. The others indicated they already had enough wisdom.

EXTENDING TO ALL LARGE LISTED COMPANIES

The following year, God had me send similar letters to the chairmen of the top 50 Australian Stock Exchange (ASX) listed companies. I did this for three more years, and then last year, He told me to send another letter to the top one hundred ASX companies, and that, I believe, completes the current task. The following is a copy of the letter I sent:

"Addressed to the Chairman

Re: Boardroom Wisdom for a successful 2012

(Please, would you pass this on to your Christian Directors)?

Dear Chairman,

"We at BRP hope that you, as Chairman of one of Australia's leading organizations, have had a successful 2011 and that you look forward to 2012 with confidence.

"We write about the critical need for an increased level of Boardroom Wisdom. Our group, Boardroom Prophets (BRP), has been helping Christian directors and owners to enhance their capacity to hear from our God and Creator for their business. We have been running this group for seven years now and have had some very supportive reports from leading listed company chairmen as well as private unlisted companies. Many of your competitor's chairmen, particularly from Asia, already understand the power of unseen forces.

"The current world of uncertainty with earthquakes, floods, and tsunamis is without precedence and clearly directors and strategists could benefit from improved insight and wisdom in their decision making. The corporate governance and directors liability environment is making it very difficult to manage companies and tends to cause risk-adverse decisions to prevail.

"Many chairmen understand the value of King Solomon's words: *"For the LORD gives wisdom, and from his mouth come knowledge and understanding"* (Prov. 2:6). *"For wisdom will enter your heart, and knowledge will be pleasant to your soul"* (Prov. 2:10). *"How much better to get wisdom than gold, to choose understanding rather than silver!"* (Prov. 16:16). *"Know also that wisdom is sweet to your soul; if you find it, there is a future hope for you, and your hope will not be cut off"* (Prov. 24:14, NIV).

"We are writing this to you and your board to encourage you to use your position and assets to maximum advantage for your shareholders and our nation. If possible, we would like you as chairman to encourage any of your directors whom you know to be Christian to seek divine wisdom and listen to God in order to receive true wisdom and wise counsel for your strategic decisions. This actually may be one of your potential competitive advantages.

"We may not believe or understand the nature of the invisible world that surrounds us, but we all know that there are things outside our control or knowledge happening every day. Some, admittedly, are natural consequences of physical laws, but others are the results of unseen systems. You may have seen that recently researchers at CERN Switzerland have identified the likely existence of fundamental particles that confirm theories of other dimensions. This may help those responsible for businesses to glimpse more of what is actually happening to them and their business.

"Please visit www.boardroomprophets.com for details.

"Thank you for your time.

"Dr. Stan Jeffery MAICD K.S.J. O.S.J. Founder, Boardroom Prophets"

We had quite a number of varied responses. One thing is clear, that listed company chairmen are quite constrained in what they can say. Clearly they cannot admit to outsiders they don't know the answers. Chairman John, who became my "advisor," told me that the letters were having a greater impact than we would ever know, as each chairman would think of this at the next board meeting.

In parallel to this, God had established the Boardroom Prophets group to help these and other directors, owners, and chairmen.

THE GROWTH OF BOARDROOM PROPHETS

The Boardroom Prophets' vision is to enable our Creator God's true wisdom to come to the boardrooms and business strategy throughout the world, starting in Sydney, to strengthen the boards' decisions!

This is to encourage and facilitate God's guidance to company boardrooms according to His will by enabling the support of Christian and other ethical directors to assist company boards and chairmen via listening to God's Holy Spirit. The model is based upon the assumption that only God knows the future and we don't, and the process is to seek His direction and guidance. This is the basis of the whole program, founded upon the promise that the Father hears His children and answers them.

Boardroom Prophets exists to create opportunities for owners and directors to receive affirmation and confirmation and confidence that the still, small voice of God can be heard (they usually already hear) and given authority over the clamor of the noise in the world. In this, we seek God's wisdom for each situation to enable us to be victorious in the world and its systems.

This, it is hoped, will ensure that our nations grow to be the best that God made them to be by creating stronger business environments via sound and successful companies. The linking together via a trusted network also provides affirmation and confirmation to all participants, including

Christian board members, chairmen, and company owners and leaders regarding what God is doing and saying.

The group is non-denominational; all those committed to or interested in being led by Jesus Christ and His Holy Spirit are welcome. We meet to strengthen the "business" body of Christ. We believe the end time harvest of 50- to 100-fold return can come to the business owners, and through them to the body of Christ as good seed put into good ground, letting God then produce the harvest.

This process of refinement is done in a supportive and encouraging environment with others who are also seeking guidance. The cooperative nature of the growth of God's wisdom is what forms the body of Christ on Earth. What is not always understood is the nature of the battle that is going on all around us—the tactics of the devil need to be exposed to enable us to be wise to the best way forward. The host company has the benefit of additional prayer and encouragement as a result of being the host for the event.

The expansion of Boardroom prophets to Melbourne and initial events in Perth, U.K., and Kenya have shown the international application of the program.

THE BOARDROOM PROPHETS' PROCESS

As the premise of Boardroom Prophets is simple, only listening to God's voice for direction and insight in business decisions, anyone can apply the principles of what we do in whatever way best fits their business or organization. This is not about Boardroom Prophets, but about releasing God's voice into our boardrooms!

However, sharing the process that we feel God has given us may help you see how to practically integrate God's voice into your business. The following is the sequence that we have been called to adopt:

- Introduction and welcome where each person speaks (this is possible because there are a small number, about 12-16 people) and breaks the ice in a comfortable way. Everyone has some idea of where everyone comes from, which aids the sharing later and formation of a trusted network.

- The communion meal is a top quality banquet and is most important as a way of unifying the body of believers into the one body, so we join together through the communion of the saints as Christ's body on earth (via the body and blood of Jesus). See Eph. 4:4, 16 to make sure we do not grieve the Holy Spirit.

- The God-at-work stage is to glorify God as He is at work in our businesses. What has He done? Where is He working? It makes sense to work with Him and praise Him for what He has done.

- Hearing from God is the culmination of the unity (communion) and the glorifying God (God at work), and this is where we listen to God for each other. Wherever two or three are gathered in His name, He is there with us. We write down what He says to help each other recognize the words we hear and recall them at a later date and pray over and into them. (Satan comes to steal these if we don't).

The use of boardrooms results in smaller numbers and the booking is easier and limited to an intimate group. It can easily be replicated to cater for growth of more people. The host business has the benefit of the special anointing and prophecy for their business.

The breakout groups of three is to facilitate God's speaking to each of us through the words and pictures from others. This should confirm and support what we may already know. This is to encourage and train us to listen and act on His still, small voice and to guide us in the boardroom, management, or other ownership meetings.

While this much of the process was successful, it became clear that we needed additional revelation on the actual strategies that Satan uses against the Christian directors in business, and in 2011, we established the Boardroom Revelations program.

THE BOARDROOM REVELATIONS PROGRAM (ALSO CALLED, "THE SUPERNATURAL SUCCESS— 'THE INVISIBLE WARFARE'")

The Boardroom Revelations program is a new program to give God the glory of enabling our businesses to see a new level of abundance and favor and give us the understanding of the way He wants us to do things. The inaugural event in 2011 was very well received and those who attended really had their area of understanding in the supernatural dimension extended. We must thank all those who gave of their time and funds to launch this program.

Our Lord God has told us to listen to the Holy Spirit for new revelation from Him. John 16:12-15 says, "'I have much more to say to you, more than you can now bear. But when he, the Spirit of truth, comes, he will guide you into all truth. He will not

speak on his own; he will speak only what he hears, and he will tell
you what is yet to come. He will bring glory to me by taking from
what is mine and making it known to you. All that belongs to the
Father is mine. That is why I said the Spirit will take from what is
mine and make it known to you'" (NIV).

The material in this program is the result of a long
personal journey. Some years ago we started praying for
ourselves and for our sons. We realized that even though
we were children of God, studied His Word, and met and
worshipped with others, there were areas of our lives that
were not fully free. Habits of the past were still a problem,
fears were holding us back, and we were generally unhappy
with our Christian walk.

The reading we had done and the teaching we had
received led us to pray in a particular way. It brought great
relief to us. When we told a leader in our church about
our experiences, he encouraged us to pray for others. This
included praying for people experiencing problems in their
business. We always kept the pastor of our church informed
of our activities. His response was, "I don't understand what
you are doing, but it seems right." He further challenged us
with the questions, "What is your scriptural basis? Where
is your fruit?" This was both helpful and challenging.
Everything we do must have its foundation in God's Word
and be examined by the fruit—the results it produces.

In 1993, we shared our experiences with a small group of
interested people. Since then we have revised the material
and shared it with many other small groups. The latest
material that was presented is aimed specifically at business
owners and those who have leadership roles in business.
We also offer a version that is aimed at those who want to

pray for their family and church members. It is our prayer that it will be helpful to you.

Over the years, much of what God has taught us and the way he has taught us to pray for people has seemed very strange. When we read Rick Joyner's book *The Final Quest*, we were amazed and encouraged. The things we had seen in prayer no longer seemed quite so strange.

We strongly recommend that you read his book. It will help you understand the reality of the battle that is going on for the hearts and souls of the people of the Earth. As you understand this battle, it is our prayer that you will be encouraged to seek out God's strength to do your part. We are the winning side and God has a role for each of us in the Final Quest.

Again, my goal here is not to draw people to myself or my organization, but to use our testimony to show how God wants to guide our decisions in life and business. Hopefully you are inspired by my story and will seek God in prayer in your business. As you do, know that each session needs to be undertaken with the Holy Spirit in control, guiding the leaders and those learning under His anointing. The Holy Spirit is the teacher of the body of Christ, so we need to allow Him to speak to us and discover the role He has for us.

BUILDING ON EARLIER FOUNDATIONS

We grew up in traditional churches, went to Sunday school, and attended religious education classes as part of the school curriculum. But we never heard about committing our lives to Jesus, praying a prayer that acknowledges our need for Jesus and asks Him to take control of our lives. It was only as adults that we heard this teaching and realized that this was what we needed and wanted. Maybe you can relate to that.

In the early years of our Christian life, we continued to attend traditional churches, but ones that taught about the Holy Spirit and encouraged the use of the gifts of the Holy Spirit. We became actively involved in the churches we attended, participating in small groups and attending and teaching in adult Sunday school classes. In addition to this, I was a member of the Full Gospel Businessmen's Fellowship. We also read books on many different topics and had meaningful conversations with friends. One area of particular interest for me was that of the effect of demonic activity. Two books left a lasting impression and affected the way in which our prayer in this area developed. They are *Demons Defeated*, by Bill Subritzky, and *The Deliverance Ministry*, by George Burch.

In *The Deliverance Ministry*, the author describes the efficacy of demanding that demons reveal their name in order to more effectively deal with them—not just a generic name, but their personal name. This is what Jesus did when he confronted the man possessed by demons at Gerasenes (Mark 5:9). We prayed for ourselves and our sons and then one evening had the opportunity to pray for a member of our church. A young lady came forward for prayer at the end of the service. It was obvious from her description of her situation that she needed the sort of prayer we had had ourselves. This needed to be done in a private place. However, as we were offering prayer for someone outside of our family, we needed permission from the leadership of the church to do so.

We approached the leader of our prayer team, unsure of the reception we would receive. God had been preparing the way. After praying for the young lady concerned, we were led on a journey of praying for people, places, and businesses. We have written a book called *Clearing the Deck,* by Stan and Jane Jeffery, which explains the way we were guided to pray and discern the strongholds in the church in Australia. These insights may also be helpful in other countries.

SHARING OUR EXPERIENCES WITH OTHERS

The first course we developed was aimed at those who wanted to pray for others in a similar way. The course was called "Yearning for More." Over six weeks, we shared our experiences, and offered participants an opportunity to be prayed for and experience the kind of praying we did. Our goal was to prepare and encourage others to take control, in the name of Jesus, of demonic activity in their lives and the lives of those close to them. Our course "Supernatural Success" takes the principles of the original course and specifically focuses on business. The purpose of both courses is not to reproduce our ways of praying in others. There is no formula, but we simply explain what has worked for us and encourage others to discover with God what will work for them.

God has great things in store for you and your business. Will you submit yourself to Him and let Him release His apostolic, prophetic voice through you to your boardroom?

ABOUT THE AUTHOR

Dr. Stan Jeffery has been a senior manager and director in the computer, software and telecommunication industry in Australia and in Europe and South East Asia for over 20 years. He has a bachelors degree in electronics from U.K. and Master of Business Administration degree from Australia (Monash), together with a Doctor of Technology degree from Deakin University specializing in early stage entrepreneurship and investment modeling. Dr. Jeffery has a background at a senior level in the blue chip companies Telstra, ICL(Fujitsu), Toshiba and Wang Labs and also running university-related commercialization and technology parks and early stage private equity and venture investment funds in Australia and South East Asia. To learn more or contact Stan, write or email him, or visit his website.

Office: Boardroom Prophets, P.O. 419 Collaroy Beach NSW 2097 Australia

Web: www.boardroomprophets.com

Email: s.jeffery@icgs.com.au

APOSTOLIC CHARACTER & MATURITY

CHAPTER THIRTY

APOSTOLIC HONOR

JOHN ANDERSON

Précis: Those who are called apostles must follow Jesus in modeling a culture of honor, and become fathers to those who would learn the way of honor.

The chapter title "Apostolic Honor" might be taken to suggest that there is a special honor to be paid to apostles by those who are not apostles. If you were hoping that to be true, you can stop reading now. In fact, Jesus declared to his apostles:

"*You will be hated by all for my name's sake*" (Matt. 10:22, Mark 13:13, Luke 21:7).

Furthermore, he predicted:

"*A disciple is not above his teacher, nor a servant above his master. It is enough for the disciple to be like his teacher, and the servant like his master. If they have called the master of the house Beelzebul, how much more will they malign those of his household*" (Matt. 10:25).

St. Paul demonstrated the fulfillment of Jesus' words, when he declared:

*"For I think that God has exhibited **us apostles as last of all**, like men sentenced to death, because we have become a spectacle to the world, to angels, and to men. We are fools for Christ's sake, but you are wise in Christ. We are weak, but you are strong. **You are held in honor, but we in disrepute**"* (1 Cor. 4:9-10, ESV, author's emphasis).

However, there is both a requirement and a reward for demonstrating proper kingdom honor where it is due. St. John writes:

"But to all who did receive him, who believed in his name, he gave the right to become children of God" (John 1:12).

The requirement is to receive him – this is Honor. The reward follows receiving him. Jesus extended the same principle when he declared:

"The one who receives a prophet because he is a prophet will receive a prophet's reward, and the one who receives a righteous person because he is a righteous person will receive a righteous person's reward" (Matt. 10:41).

Jesus declared: *"Truly, truly, I say to you, whoever receives the one I send receives me, and whoever receives me receives the one who sent me"* (John 13:20, Matt. 10:40, Luke 9:48).

HONOR CASE STUDY

In 1997, a fellow executive announced his departure from Weyerhaeuser Company to pursue a new career. Departing employees typically are honored with one 'going-away party,' but groups from across the company held eight separate gatherings to offer going-away presents, and to honor his contributions to the company. He was the leader of a small corporate staff, not a division officer or CEO. He had only served at the company for four years. Why all of the fuss? Some of the comments made at his departure parties included:

"When [he] was hired, I resented it. I had served for 25 years, paid my dues. I had earned the MBA and demonstrated my leadership. But here came this young hotshot from Sprint, taking the position that was rightfully mine. I think that he sensed my resentment, but instead of retaliation, he offered me the one thing I needed to succeed: respect. He honored my service, listened to my ideas, refined my approach and opened doors that were previously closed to me. He set the example of honor for all of us." (CTO)

"Weyerhaeuser is a great company to work for, but no one is accepted as part of the culture until they have been here a long time. It takes about 20 years just to know who is who in the zoo. But [he] worked hard, and in a few months became a more articulate spokesman for the company, its culture, its values, and its greatness than anyone I have worked with. His name was always on the list of those we consider ambassadors." (Senior Executive)

I interviewed this executive to see what was behind the accolades. During his brief four-year tenure, his subordinates received Annual President's Awards four separate times. These awards, which include cash, stock, and other public recognition, had always been given to division P&L leaders. He talked openly about his staff returning $4 to the company in hard cost savings for each $1 spent, about helping instill a new writing style across the company, to reengineer corporate policy deployment so that each division and department could function autonomously while preserving a common set of values, and to implement new technology commercialization processes to keep R&D focused and relevant. It seems that this humble leader touched the entire company in a few brief years. What gave him such access?

During our talk, he candidly discussed the effort he had made to learn the culture and history of the company. The more he had learned, the more he discovered what was worthy of honor. He related this story to me:

"I discovered that the company had a library and a professional archivist. She knew where everything was and when it was added to the collection. I told her my desire to be an honorable leader, and asked if she would design a comprehensive program for me. Each evening, I would stop by her desk and retrieve a new file box of materials. Inside were 4-6 hours of corporate videos, some articles, reports, advertisements and so on. I would take it home for review, and return it in the morning. This continued for about 3 months. During that time, I saw every advertisement, facilities review, executive communiqué, Total Quality Management team report, newspaper article and analyst review written during the last 40 years of the company's 100-year history. My motivation was not to become an expert in company history, but to 'give honor where honor is due.'"

The honor he demonstrated to others was returned to him, with access to the company's leaders and in being included in efforts to address its major problems. He honored the company, he honored his staff, and the company's leaders. At his departure, they returned the honor to him. You may be wondering how this story relates to our chapter title, "Apostolic Honor." That young executive is a commissioned Apostle of Jesus Christ. He intentionally modeled, practiced and demonstrated honor at work, making an impact and lasting impression on all who knew him.

JESUS IS OUR MODEL OF HONOR

Jesus, the first Apostle, is the model of Kingdom Honor. Those who are called apostles must follow Jesus in living a culture of honor. But Jesus did not learn the culture of Honor from his earthly experience alone, but in union with his Father in Heaven. In the familiar discussion with Nicodemus, Jesus remarked:

"Truly, truly, I say to you, we speak of what we know, and bear witness to what we have seen, but you do not receive our testimony. If I have told you earthly things and you do not believe, how can you believe if I tell you heavenly things? No one has ascended into heaven except he who descended from heaven, the Son of Man" (John 3:11-13, ESV).

It is on the basis of Jesus' experience in Heaven that he tells us to pray:

"Your kingdom come, your will be done, on earth as it is in heaven" (Matt. 6:10).

Jesus learned everything from His Father, declaring: "I *only do what I see my father doing"* (John 5:19, ESV). This means that Jesus learned honor by watching – and receiving honor, from the Father. Jesus and His Father honored one another. Jesus declared:

"I honor my Father" (John 8:49, ESV).

Peter was a witness of at least one incident where the Father verbally honored Jesus in the presence of witnesses:

"…. he [Jesus] received honor and glory from God the Father, and the voice was borne to him by the Majestic Glory, 'This is my beloved Son, with whom I am well pleased'" (2 Pet. 1:17, ESV).

Was this honor reserved for Jesus alone, or does the Father seek to bring honor to men who please Him? Scripture makes it very plain that the Father delights to show honor to honorable men.

"How can you believe, who receive honor from one another, and do not seek the honor that comes from the only God?" (John 5:44, NKJV).

"Those who honor me I will honor, and those who despise me shall be lightly esteemed" (1 Sam. 2:30, ESV).

"...the LORD bestows favor and honor" (Ps. 84.11, ESV).

HOW DID THE FATHER HONOR JESUS?

He gave Jesus:

- **Glory** (John 17:21, John 8:54)
- **Intimacy** (John 8:55)
- **Words** (John 8:26-28)
- **Miraculous Works** (John 5:36)
- **Authority** (John 17:2)
- **Judgment** (John 5:27)

In addition to the things above, Jesus arranged the timing and affairs of the world in such a way that hundreds of prophecies, spoken thousands of years in advance, were accurately fulfilled with absolutely no action taken by Jesus to assist their performance.

The Father initiated the relationship, and Jesus responded to the Father's initiative. This means that in childhood, when Father wooed him, Jesus responded just as Samuel did when sleeping in the Tabernacle courts. Only by responding to the Father, could Jesus declare, *"I do nothing on my own initiative."* Had it been otherwise, Jesus might have urged his followers to have a strategy, follow a plan, and try harder!

Jesus was intimate with the Father, declaring *"I and the Father are one,"* and *"If you have seen me you have seen the Father."* He could boldly state: *"If you knew the Father, then you would love me, for he sent me."*

In *Abba's Child*, Brennan Manning declares that "abba" (daddy) is the greatest revelation of God (YHWH) ever spoken by Jesus – far surpassing all else that he said. Jesus urges us to pray "Our abba...in Heaven." Abba flutters off of a baby's lips, uttered without guile, in unashamed intimacy while in the arms of the one who sired you, desired you, who protects and provides for you, and who longs to bring you into an awareness of your identity so that you can fulfill your destiny. As a baby, Jesus cried to his Abba, and Abba took him into his arms and began connecting him with his identify and destiny. By the time Nicodemus came looking for private tutoring at night, Jesus could calmly ask, *"If I have told you earthly things and you do not believe, how can you believe if I tell you heavenly things?"* (John 3:12). This intimacy is honor.

In giving Jesus works to fulfill and accomplish, coupled with the authority to heal the sick, expel demons, change water to wine, calm the seas, quiet the storm, and walk on water, the Father ensured that Jesus was unmistakably marked as a Prince sent by the King! This, too, is honor.

The Father transfigures Jesus, brings Moses and Elijah through time to meet with the Son, and parts the heavens yet again to audibly declare His fatherhood of and His pleasure with Jesus. This glory is Father showing honor to the Son.

How does a man honor God? Can he enrich him with Gold, shower him with Glory, promote him with a powerful public relations campaign, or elect him or his chosen ones to some office carrying great authority? Can he mount up and conduct an armed campaign to eradicate God's enemies? If one were to watch many "religious broadcasts," (irrespective of the religion) one could be convinced that in fact all of these things do honor God. But do they?

Hebrews declares that, *"The Son is the radiance of God's glory and the exact representation of his being."* Jesus models Kingdom Honor for the Father, as well as honor for other people. Let's look first at how Jesus honors the Father.

HOW JESUS HONORS THE FATHER

King Xerxes I, when he had determined that Mordecai the Jew had not yet been honored for disclosing a plot to kill the King, asked his advisor: *"What should be done to the man whom the king delights to honor?"* (Est. 6:6, ESV). The King was wise enough to know that you can only show true honor to one whom you know quite well. One man may receive honor from a soft word of thanks spoken in person, while another might delight in a public feast, and yet another might wish for riches or being promoted to a position of authority. Conversely, the one who seeks authority might feel snubbed by a quiet word of thanks.

Likewise, Jesus pays careful attention to the Father to know what is important to Him. Many times, his statements reveal that the motive for his actions are grounded solely in a desire to Honor the Father. Prophetically speaking,

Isaiah declared that the Messiah would *"take delight in the Fear of The Lord, and make righteous decisions for the poor and oppressed"* (Isa. 11:4-5, NIV). The phrase "take delight" is a form of the Hebrew "ruach" (wind, breath, or spirit) that means to "snort" or "inhale" like a steed trying to catch the scent of battle. The word picture is that Messiah would be "sniffing out the fear of the Lord" – just as the Father sniffs out the aroma of the sacrifice that attracts his presence. Wherever the Father goes, the fear of the LORD manifests in his presence. So, Jesus is always seeking to discern, to detect, the Presence by "sniffing the Fear of the Lord." When he is in the Presence, he makes righteous judgments for the poor and oppressed.

What are the other ways in which Jesus demonstrates honor for the Father?

- **Imitation.** Jesus commands us, *"You must therefore be perfect, as your heavenly Father is perfect,"* (Matt. 5:48, ESV), and then declared his own passionate pursuit: *"whoever has seen me has seen the Father"* (John 14:9). How many of us can say that?

- **Intimacy.** The Father initiated the pursuit of intimacy, but Jesus responded with passionate devotion. As a result, he was able to declare, *"I and the Father are one"* (John 10:30, ESV). This intimacy is evidenced by Jesus' comfort in making promises for the Father to keep! For example, *"If anyone loves me, he will keep my word, and my Father will love him, and we will come to him and make our home with him"* (John 14:23, ESV), or even *"In that day you will ask nothing of me. Truly, truly, I say to you, whatever* *you ask of the Father in my name, he will give it to you"* (John 16:23, ESV).

- **Radical Obedience.** Jesus knows the Father's character, and trusts all His motives for fulfilling his Son's destiny. As a result, he can fully obey. *"I have kept my Father's commandments and abide in his love"* (John 15:10, ESV). This honors the Father.

- **Stewardship.** The Father gave many things to Jesus, including each of his disciples. Jesus then gave them back to him, declaring his mission was to lead them to The Father: *"I am the way, and the truth, and the life. No one comes to the Father except through me"* (John 14:6). In his final prayer before crucifixion, Jesus plugged them into the Father in the same way that Jesus was plugged in – the Glory! He prayed for his followers *"that they may all be one, just as you, Father, are in me, and I in you, that they also may be in us, so that the world may believe that you have sent me"* (John 17:21, ESV). An owner always reserves something for himself, but a steward returns all that was given to the one whose it truly is. Stewardship honors the Father.

So, we have The Model for Honor: The Father Honors the Son. The Son Honors the Father.

HOW DOES JESUS HONOR US?

If we learn that, we'll know how to honor one another by imitating His example.

First, the Honor is tailor-made to each one. Just like Xerxes I asking, *"What shall be done for the man whom the King delights to honor?"*, Jesus knows us intimately. He understands how we are wired, and what expression of honor truly is refreshing and life changing for us.

I recently was asked to complete a thorough personality profile, with over 250 questions. When the report was returned to my leadership coach, he exclaimed, "You have the LOWEST need for attention and affirmation of anyone who has ever taken this test!" Now he knows why I do not respond to praise and promises of increased popularity. He also noted that I am "challenge driven" and have a knack for bringing order in chaotic situations. For me, Honor means getting assigned a gnarly, complex problem that is too daunting for others.

Secondly, the Honor is connected to our destiny. The One who had more thoughts about us than the sands of the sea before the foundation of the world, knows the plan for our life. He also knows how we are wired, and what additional preparation is required so that we can succeed at each step along the path. For some of us, honor means being introduced to a great coach, while for others, it is being given a great challenge.

I have personally witnessed acts of lavish generosity by some Apostles, who have given cars, jeweled swords, money, and public acclamation to men and women of exceptional heritage and kingdom character. In each case, these acts have brought unity, reconciliation, and released the Presence of God into the lives of those present. These men have truly set the pace for the saints, modeling Heaven's honor for the lives and deeds of those who were called out.

Recently I slid into the only seat left open at the impromptu concert held at a friend's barn. The seat was beside a large, loud, hairy, man wearing a tie-died tee-shirt. He had been sent to bring 3rd-heaven support to the 24 hour x 30 day live worship 'Burn' that we had launched – covering the entire state from five worship centers ('furnaces'). With tears in my eyes, I embraced him and said, "Thank you for coming. Thank you for paying the price you paid to obey the Lord. You are welcome in our town and in our hearts."

Between songs, Papa John told me his story. He had been sent to 48 states on a mission: bring intercessory repentance to the sites where revival fires once burned brightly, but now weren't even smoldering: Cane Ridge, Kentucky; Azusa Street, California, etc. Before leaving, Papa John held numerous meetings in which spectacular miracles occurred, and was granted a vision in which our regional leadership ministry was featured prominently in the Lord's prophetic destiny for the Northwest and beyond. In the final meeting before his departure, Papa John remarked that being received with humility and honor opened the way for his ministry to be effective. Jesus said, *"Anyone who receives you receives me."*

CONCLUSION

In closing, my favorite apostle, St. Paul, challenged his readers to *"Outdo one another in showing honor,"* *"manage your body with honor,"* *"Honor widows,"* *"Honor the King,"* *Honor all Men"* and *"Honor those who suffer for the gospel."*

Apostles are to set an example of properly honoring others, not in being honored. In fact, in 1 Cor 4.10, Paul confessed, *"You are held in honor, but we are held in disrepute,"* and then *"death works in us, but life in you"* (2 Cor. 4:12, ESV).

This chapter has focused on the need for Apostles to model giving kingdom honor to others. But, is there a place for providing special honor to Apostles? In principle, Jesus declared, *"Truly, truly, I say to you, whoever receives the one I send receives me, and whoever receives me receives the one who sent me"* (John 13:20, ESV).

Finally, Paul declares, *"For I think that God has exhibited us apostles as last of all, like men sentenced to death, because we have become a spectacle to the world, to angels, and to men"* (1 Cor. 4:9, ESV). Beware of men who seek to be honored because they are Apostles, but be imitators of those who are generous in honoring others in a way that displays an intimate understanding of their heart, and a godly reverence for their destiny.

ABOUT THE AUTHOR

John Anderson is a husband (married 36 years to Mary Ann Roe), father of two sons (Jeremy and James), grandfather of two splendid baby girls, and is a spiritual son of Dr. Bruce Cook. Apostolically, he is co-leading a community and regional transformation project in concert with a local council, and travels internationally to minister forgiveness, healing and reconciliation. Professionally, John is the Founder and CEO of Global Development Partners Ltd., a venture focused on empowering at-risk communities globally to achieve viable infrastructures and sustainable economies. He also serves as an advisor to a ranking member of the U.S. Congress, several boards of directors, and a couple of life coaches.

John's experience includes multiple assignments as a CEO, CIO, CTO, CQO, and COO in high tech ventures ranging from biotechnology, e-commerce, homeland defense/counterterrorism, and energy. Previously he advised Governors, Generals, University Provosts, and CEOs of numerous Global 2000 companies. He has earned a BS in Physics, *summa cum laude* (Ohio U.) and an MBA in Marketing, *magna cum laude* (U. of Ky.), and is a member of *Who's Who in International Executives* and *Who's Who in Information Technology*. John's life Scripture is: *"Can a country be born in a day or a nation be brought forth in a moment?"* (Isa. 66:8).

CHAPTER THIRTY-ONE

APOSTOLIC INTEGRITY

MARK HENDERSON

For about a 10-year period, from the mid-1970s to the mid-1980s, I was involved with an apostolic ministry on the West Coast of the U.S. which planted about 65 churches. We had six ordained apostles and at one point in the early 1980s, they decided to host conferences based on each of the five-fold ministry gifts listed in Eph. 4:11, for equipping and impartation. It was my understanding that a person could only attend one of these conferences if the leaders felt like they were called to the particular office being highlighted. I was invited to attend the "Prophets Conference" because they thought that I might be called to the office of a prophet. Interestingly, instead of receiving confirmation to a prophetic calling, I actually received the first prophetic confirmation to my apostolic calling at the conference, but I learned a lot nonetheless, and felt honored to be there as a young leader.

All six of the ordained apostles were there and two or three well known, seasoned prophets had been invited from other ministries to teach and impart to the prophets and prophets-in-training in our ministry. One of the highlights of the conference was when one or more of the guest prophets started to prophesy over one of our main leaders who was in attendance at the conference. This apostle was the leader who had planted the largest church in our ministry in Central America and I can still picture the prophecy being given because the anointing was so strong! Part of the content of the prophecy was that the Lord was indicating that the sphere of influence of this man's work was going to greatly expand into all of Central America. The Lord was promoting him to a new level because he had been faithful in what God had already given him.

Another aspect of the conference that impacted me greatly was when the highest level prophetess in our ministry, who was also the founding apostle's wife, delivered a public prophetic Word to the attendees of the conference, which was a fairly small group of around a hundred people. I had been struggling with an area of secret sin that none of my fellow leaders knew about before the conference and I had privately prayed that the Lord would deliver me from it because it had happened a few times and I couldn't seem to get the victory over it. So, during the prophetic Word that this prophetess released, which seemed to last from between about 15 minutes to half an hour, the Lord intermingled Words of Knowledge in which secret sin was described for several people at the conference, including me.

She had not named names, but the descriptions of the sins were very specific so that everyone affected by the prophecy knew in their spirit that this Word was referring to them! It was awesome—but also very frightening because I knew that the Lord had "read my mail," through this prophetess. Immediately after the prophecy, the founding apostle stood up and said to the group that if anyone's sin had been revealed during the prophecy that they should not leave the meeting without repenting of the sin. So, he and the other six apostles stood up in front of the congregation, so that all of us who had had our sin revealed would have an opportunity to repent, if we were obedient, and bold enough to do so.

I had been crying out for the Lord to heal me of that area of secret sin, so He chose to do it in that way. I remember sweating profusely as I left my seat to go up front to repent of the sin I was so ashamed of. I was under "prophetic arrest," so to speak, so the only way out was to be obedient and repent. I realize now that I could have ignored the opportunity to go forward and probably no one else in the room would have even known that my sin had just been exposed. However, the Lord had made it very clear to me, also in the wording of the prophecy, that there would be very serious consequences for my ministry should I choose to not repent of the sin in that specific way!

So, being in attendance in the conference had suddenly changed from being one of the most special things that had happened to me at that point in my ministry, because it had been such an honor to be invited to such an event, to then being one of the most humiliating things that had ever happened to me, because now all of these seasoned leaders would see my secret sin being exposed!

I chose to repent to the apostle that had received the powerful prophetic Words about Central America, so I confessed my sin to him—very quietly, I might add, because I was so ashamed. So, this apostle led me in a quiet prayer of very serious repentance, and then he delivered a Word of prophecy to me that literally changed my life in the area in which I had been struggling. The prophecy was a Word of restoration as to how the Lord was going to change me so that I could have victory in that area of my life. I believe that that prophetic Word has changed my life more than any other Word I have ever received in reference to learning how to deal with sin! So, what I believe I received at that conference was a type of prophetic surgery, in which the Lord Himself first exposed my sin and then spoke to me directly as to how He was going to heal me. It was awesome, and I encourage anyone who may be reading this book, that if you are ever placed under prophetic arrest, like I was, in reference to an area of secret sin, or even if you are feeling conviction from the Holy Spirit, as you are reading this right now, to simply yield to the opportunity and confess your sins and allow the Lord to heal you in the way that He sees fit.

INTEGRITY IS REQUIRED OF APOSTLES

You might be wondering how the story that I just shared relates to my understanding for the need of apostolic integrity? Firstly, now that I, too, am a recognized apostle, I'm very thankful that the Lord "nipped it in the bud," in reference to that area of secret sin that had slipped into my life when I was still a young leader, having yet to be ordained into my five-fold calling.

Secondly, and ironically, the very same ordained apostle who had planted the fastest-growing church in our ministry in Central America, who was used of the Lord in my healing at that conference, later fell into sexual immorality with a church secretary, and left his family! He had to be removed from the ministry, and the church was turned over to other leaders! About 20 years ago, I remember seeing an article in *Charisma Magazine* in which that particular church was mentioned as being one of the fastest-growing churches in all of Central America, now having planted over 100 churches from that original church plant. So, the prophesies that I had heard spoken over the apostle's life did actually come to pass with the ministry that he had started, but because of the sin of sexual immorality, he actually missed out on the blessings of being involved with the work that the Lord had intended for him to oversee!

There are varying estimates of the number of apostles in the New Testament, but almost the entire New Testament was written by them, and the largest portion was written by the apostle Paul, who had not even been one of the original 12 disciples of Christ. In this group of the first true apostles of the Lord, there was never sexual immorality named among them! And, only one time was financial immorality named among them, and that was in the case of Judas Iscariot. In reference to Judas, the book of Acts records:

"And they prayed and said, 'You, O Lord, who know the hearts of all, show which of these two You have chosen to take part in **this ministry and apostleship from which Judas by transgression fell**, *that he might go to his own place.' And they cast their lots, and the lot fell on Matthias. And he was numbered with the eleven apostles"* (Acts 1:24-26, NKJV, author's emphasis).

So, in accordance with Acts 1:25, Judas Iscariot lost his office of apostleship by sinning! One can't "fall" from something that they have never possessed. So, Judas Iscariot had obviously been a true apostle, but what "transgression" caused Judas to fall? We know that Judas betrayed the Lord, so the sin of betrayal was obviously the most serious sin that he committed, but why did Judas betray Jesus? I believe that it was immorality in the area of finances that led to Judas' betrayal of Jesus.

Judas obviously had a measure of faith when he responded to the call of Jesus, by forsaking everything, to become one of the 12 disciples of the Lord. His faith probably grew by leaps and bounds when he fully participated with the other apostles during the times Jesus sent them out two by two to preach the gospel, to cast out demons and to heal the sick! Judas witnessed firsthand the raising of the dead, Jesus walking on the water, turning the water into wine, etc., so he must have known that Jesus was a holy man of God, at the very least a prophet. It is apparent that the faith of all of the apostles was growing in a similar way during their incredibly special time of getting to be with Jesus for three-and-a-half years.

So, what was different about Judas as compared to the other apostles? Judas had a "secret," of which there is no reference in the Bible that he ever acknowledged or repented. The secret sin of Judas, which only Jesus knew about by the Spirit, was the sin of stealing money from the money bag. This is referenced in John 12:6, in the situation where Judas revealed the sin in his heart by questioning Jesus' decision to allow Mary to wash His feet with her hair and a very expensive oil of spikenard. Judas said the oil could have been sold and used to feed the poor, while secretly only desiring more money to come in, so that he could steal more!

Judas was present when the rich young ruler approached Jesus in Mark 10:17, and asked what he must do to inherit eternal life. Judas heard Jesus say to the man, *"You know the commandments,"* in verse 19, which included, *"Do not steal."* The rich young ruler replied, *"Teacher, all these things I have kept from my youth."* Judas Iscariot then heard Jesus say to this man in verse 21, *"One thing you lack: Go your way, sell whatever you have and give to the poor, and you will have treasure in heaven; and come, take up the cross, and follow Me."*

And finally, Judas witnessed the man go away sorrowfully because he had great possessions.

Judas was also present when Jesus said the following:

"'No servant can serve two masters; for either he will hate the one and love the other, or else he will be devoted to one and despise the other. You cannot serve God and wealth.' Now the Pharisees, who were lovers of money, were listening to all these things and were scoffing at Him" (Luke 16:13-14, NASB).

So, Judas Iscariot was without excuse in reference to his financial immorality at every level! Jesus had clearly stated in many ways to His disciples that stealing and loving money were totally unacceptable practices! Judas obviously had those many opportunities to repent to Jesus and to come clean of his secret sin and change his evil ways, but chose not to. Therefore, because Judas persisted in loving money rather than God, and thinking he could get away with his sin and no one would ever know or find out about it, Satan entered into him, as is recorded in Luke 22:3, and Judas plotted with the chief priests to betray Jesus for 30 pieces of the unrighteous silver that Judas so loved, esteemed and coveted.

After Jesus was betrayed by a kiss from Judas, taken prisoner, tortured and condemned to be crucified, Judas desperately tried to make things right when he realized what he had done, but it was too late, as is recorded in the following passage:

"Then Judas, His betrayer, seeing that He had been condemned, was remorseful and brought back the thirty pieces of silver to the chief priests and elders, saying, 'I have sinned by betraying innocent blood.' And they said, 'What is that to us? You see to

it!' Then he threw down the pieces of silver in the temple and departed, and went and hanged himself" (Matt. 27:3-5, NKJV).

The following quote from an unknown author rings so true: "Sin will take you further than you want to go. It will keep you longer than you want to stay, and it will cost you more than you want to pay." The life of Judas Iscariot stands as a firm reminder and warning to all of us who are committed to seeing the integrity of the apostolic office fully restored. May we all quickly repent when necessary and walk in the ways of Jesus, the Chief Apostle of the Faith!

CONCLUSION

I like this insight from Jonas Clark: "Judas was an apostle who walked with Jesus. He saw the feeding of the multitudes, the dead raised, and lepers cleansed. He heard glorious words of everlasting life. Yet, he is listed over and over again in the gospels and remembered throughout history as the one 'who sought opportunity to betray him.'"[1] This reference is from Matt. 26:16. Clark also noted: "Judas, although numbered among the apostles, did not act in a heated moment of passion. He was very calculating and cunning as he betrayed the Lord. He even sank so low as to lead the Roman soldiers to where Jesus was (Acts 1:16)."[2]

None of us is above or beyond the temptation and seduction of sin – not even an apostle. We must all take heed and guard our hearts and minds lest we stumble and fall (Ps. 39:1, Luke 21:34, 1 Tim. 4:16, 1 Cor. 10:12, Heb. 3:12, Acts 20:28, 2 Cor. 10:3-5). Let this example of Judas, a true apostle who became deceived and fell into sin and death (see Jas. 1:13-15), be a warning and a reminder to us all.

ENDNOTES

1. Jonas Clark, *Governing Churches & Antioch Apostles: Discovering the New Apostolic Reformation*, p. 253. Hallandale, FL: Spirit of Life Publishing, 2000.

2. Ibid.

ABOUT THE AUTHOR

Mark Henderson is apostolic overseer of Glory House Christian Center in Austin, Texas. He has served in Christian ministry for over 30 years including domestic and foreign missions work, involving planting churches and equipping the saints through the five-fold as well as in prophetic, apostolic, evangelistic, intercession, worship, healing and deliverance ministries with an emphasis on moral character, sound doctrine, and signs and wonders. Mark is currently writing a book on eschatology and serves on several boards. He is married and has one grown daughter. To learn more or contact Mark, visit The Glory House web site at www.gloryhouse.net.

CHAPTER THIRTY-TWO

APOSTOLIC MANTLES: THE PRICE TO PAY

DR. MICHELLE A. MORRISON

THE CALL

In this age of reformation and revolution, the Lord has been training and preparing the five-fold ministry for the greatest Awakening to ever hit the face of the earth. In Eph. 4, verses 11 and 12, the Bible states:

"And he gave some, apostles; and some, prophets; and some, evangelists; and some, pastors and teachers; For the perfecting of the saints, for the work of the ministry, for the edifying of the body of Christ."

I recall coming up in ministry and often being taught that "the anointing costs." After having my own ministry now for over a decade, I have truly "experienced" the full meaning of that phrase. Many times baby Christians receive prophetic words about their callings or mantles and mistakenly believe that that this is a "now" word. I've heard many express desires to attend conferences so that they can "pick up mantles." While I do believe in impartation (2 Tim. 1:6), I have come to realize that in order for Christians to truly walk in our mantles with "power," there is a process. Some individuals can and do walk in a certain level of "power" after an impartation, but if our character has not been developed, the enemy will come in and destroy our lives:

"Not a novice, lest being lifted up with pride he fall into the condemnation of the devil" (1 Tim. 3:6).

I do believe God releases some to walk in offices or mantles after a shorter testing period than others, depending on our levels of obedience. But, I've learned from the Word, experience, and renewed revelation from the Holy Spirit, that God is never in a hurry, and that He must take us through so many trials to truly test our hearts and prepare us.

PREPARATION

The Lord prepared Moses over a time period of 40 years in the wilderness (Acts 7:29-30). In Exodus 2, we see God's chosen leader not ready for his mantle. He operated in the flesh and not by the Spirit and tried to take destiny into his own hands. Wanting to deliver his people, Moses committed murder and killed an Egyptian slave-master. The Lord then had to place him in the desert of Midian, for 40 long years. If God had not allowed Moses to be processed during this period, he would not have been humble enough to follow God's instructions before Pharaoh, and would not have become familiar with the same desert through which he would later lead the Israelites.

Forty years is a long time. Moses went from carrying a revolutionary mantle while in his royal Egyptian position, to becoming nothing. During that long wilderness period, Moses more than likely lived in doubt about his true destiny and calling. He more than likely felt like his life was at a standstill – that the dream of delivering his people would never come to pass. But this period of separation was necessary to teach him humility. God stripped him of his royal mantle, and thereby taught him self-abasement. While Moses may have felt like his vision had died, God allowed this period so that he could work on this leader's character.

He also placed Moses in this environment to prepare him to lead the children of Israel through that same location once delivered from Egypt. So many times, we do not understand the seasons in our lives. I believe over the last several years God has had the Body of Christ on a standstill. Some have wondered if the prophetic words they were given years back would ever come to pass. But my friends, I am here to tell you that God has been working. While He has been preparing the character of the Body, He has also strategically been positioning us in places connected to our true callings and purposes. Many tried to force God's hands by operating in the flesh and charting their own courses. But, God had to divinely intervene and stall our plans. His purposes will be unveiled in time, if they have not already been revealed to you. Now is the time and the season. And when we see the end result, we will be glad that the process occurred.

Moses was unaware that God was transforming him into his true identity during the wilderness season of his life. He probably thought to himself that he had lost his position of royalty to now look after sheep, but actually, he had been gaining inner treasures that could not have been reaped from his prior role. The Bible admonishes us in Matt. 6, verses 19-20:

"Lay not up for yourselves treasures upon earth, where moth and rust doth corrupt, and where thieves break through and steal: But lay up for yourselves treasures in heaven, where

neither moth nor rust doth corrupt, and where thieves do not break through nor steal..."

The Body of Christ has been in a preparation or wilderness period over the past several years and has been storing up heavenly treasures. Some have thought to themselves that there has been so much talk of the coming revival for years now. "When Lord, when?" has been the cry. But, everything must happen in God's perfect timing. If you are like me, God has taught you humility, mercy and selflessness during this past season. Those character traits cannot be bought with gold. He has shown me so much mercy that I have to now extend that same mercy to others.

Only through the passing of God's tests and trials can we ever hope to be like Him, the One full of so much grace that He sacrificed His life for us. Until we get to that place where we are willing to lay down our agendas for the cause of the gospel, then we are not ready – we are not prepared for our mantles. Some of us have been so focused on our seemingly stagnant places, that we have lost sight of the ways of God. He says His ways are far above our ways (Isa. 5:9).

God tested Abraham by asking him to sacrifice the son he had waited for through many difficult years—the child of his old age. This was the "son of promise." But, Abraham knew God's ways, and obeyed (Gen. 22:6). Because of his faith and obedience, Abraham was qualified to receive his inheritance. The Lord has asked some of us to sacrifice the "promise" He has given to us. For some, it was that successful business that would allow them to go into ministry full-time without worry; for others, it was that calling that was going to "revolutionize the world." Some have instead seen one failure after the next, in both business and church ministry. It seems like every venture has folded, every program has failed. But, we must understand that it is the Lord who has allowed our plans to fall through or to be placed on shelves for a time. God will ask us to do some of the most difficult things in order for us to obtain our true anointings, but the choice will be up to us whether we obey. We need to understand that God is not a man that He should lie (Num. 23-19). He who began a good work in us will complete it (Phil. 1:6).

REVEALING OF THE SONS OF GOD

The time is near when He will fully reveal the "sons of God" (Rom. 8:19) to the world. The Bible tells us that the whole creation waits eagerly for the revelation of the promise that He has given to us. And, each individual must fulfill his or her own calling. There is no need to worry about someone else fulfilling that promise because God has anointed each one specifically for an assignment. I believe we would have less jealousy in the Body if we would accept this truth. Try as they might, others cannot fulfill what God has called us to do. He will place us in the right place and at the right time for our dreams to successfully unfold.

The Word of God is given for instruction, correction and training in righteousness (2 Tim. 3:16). As with these great leaders in the Bible, the Lord must prepare us (sometimes through hard trials) for our offices or mantles.

I have known for some time that the Lord called me to walk in the office of an apostle. However, over the last several years, the Lord, I believe, stripped me, cleansed me, poured me out, to re-fill me with an even greater anointing. I saw great healings in our ministry years ago. But, the Lord subsequently instructed me that I had to change the direction of our traditional Church because "I" had birthed it and that "Ishmael" had to die in order for "Isaac" to come forth. I then set out on a course of consecration before the Lord to find out His perfect will; this is the period I call my wilderness years.

Like Moses, for years it seemed as if the calling had been stalled as I worked heavy hours in Manhattan's law firms as a contract attorney. Little did I know that through these divinely-placed assignments, He would give me part of the blueprint for the city and nation.

During this process, and before the Lord released me into my full apostolic office, He gave me a revelatory dream concerning apostolic callings. The dream showed the danger in picking up full mantles before we are ready, or before God fully shapes our characters. I recall a flood coming down from heaven in the dream. Suddenly, I found myself in the flood waters. I cannot swim and the tidal waves were so high that they could have enveloped me. I looked to the side and saw a preacher helplessly being carried away by the water downstream. She was waving for help, but I could not swim and she was so far away. Somehow I was sure she had drowned in the flood. I was miraculously able to stay afloat, although not a swimmer.

After some time the water subsided. I found myself then standing on acres of land seemingly in an upscale neighborhood. I rang the bell of what appeared to be a mansion on the property. A lady with blonde hair greeted me after opening the door. She seemed to have been expecting me. I saw that she was carrying a large metal bed-head frame which was covered in gold. I somehow knew this was my gift, but when I reached for it she told me to wait. She said that if I tried to carry it before the right time, I would die. I knew what she was trying to say. It seemed as if the flood waters had injured me and I still needed to recover in my mind. She instructed me to continue on my pathway and pick the bed-head up in the right time. We both knew I had to go through more flood territory but she gave me some medicine which seemed to refresh me right away. But, I knew I was not completely healed at that time.

The Lord showed me clearly that this mantle in the dream represented not just the office He had called me to, but apostolic mantles in the Body of Christ as a whole. This is why the frame seemed so heavy and was the "head" portion of the bed. Of course, the gold represents Kingdom wealth, which the Body will be entrusted with. He therefore wanted to take the Body of Christ through a cleansing process before we could walk in the level of anointing and authority necessary to win the war against Satan.

If we recall, Elisha in the Bible had to lay hold of his mantle several times. The first mantle he received while working in the field, when Elijah passed by and threw his cloak upon him (1 Kings 19:19). The final mantle came when he passed the test of not leaving the side of the man of God and being at the right place and the right time to see Elijah being taken up into heaven in a chariot (2 Kings 2:11-14).

Elijah had tested Elisha by asking him to turn back from following him. In fact, he had done this several times. But, Elisha was so in tune with God and his timing that he refused. In the same way, we must spend time with God so we are aware of the seasons. We must never turn back or give up, no matter how much it seems like we can't seem to lay hold of that which the Lord has promised. Those offices may even be marketplace callings. We must press through to get our blessings. We need to be so in tune with God. His perfect will comes only by spending time with Him. He is a God of timing. When we spend time with Him, then He will show us where to go and what to do to possess our inheritances—to lay hold of them, as in my dream mentioned earlier. I had, like Elisha, received the first phase of the mantle several years earlier, but I had to be prepared for the full measure of the office I would walk in.

ENDURANCE IS DEVELOPED, NOT IMPARTED

He also revealed that there were tests (mostly relating to my job) that I had to pass in my wilderness season before picking up my true mantle. I had, in fact, been enduring trials of persecution (and sometimes failure at what I thought was God's will for ministry), in my wilderness. I had let those tests, especially the one right before I had the dream, affect my mind. However, I had learned to maybe endure better than some leaders in their trials; some had been disqualified or had even died in their situations (symbolized by the water carrying away the pastor). I had made it to this point, where the trials had subsided (one particularly challenging trial had just ended), and He was showing me the mantle (the bed-head) at the end of the journey, to encourage me.

I believe the blonde lady in the dream was a minister whose service I attended in New Jersey after one particularly challenging test. The word she gave, that God wanted to give us new hearts of love, helped to heal the wounds of the past season. As I was in that service, I immediately felt all of the resentment over the wrong I had suffered melt away when she ministered about laying down our lives for the King and becoming laid-down lovers. However, I knew that a part of my mind was still deeply affected by my experiences, and that I would need more healing before coming into my true calling. The Lord gave me the following scriptures to support the interpretation of my dream and to encourage me to not give up and to finish the course:

"Thou hast caused men to ride over our heads; we went through fire and through water: but thou broughtest us out into a wealthy place" (Ps. 66:12, KJV).

"When the waves of death compassed me, the floods of ungodly men made me afraid;... In my distress I called upon the Lord, and cried to my God: and he did hear my voice out of his temple, and my cry did enter into his ears. Then the earth shook and trembled: the foundations of the heavens moved and shook, because he was wroth. There went up a smoke out of his nostrils, and fire out of his mouth devoured: coals were kindled by it. He bowed the heavens also, and came down, and darkness was under his feet. And he rode upon a cherub and did fly: and he was sent upon the wings of the wind... He delivered me from my strong enemy, and from them that hated me: for they were too strong for me... He brought me forth also into a large place..." (2 Sam. 22: 5, 7-11, 18, 20).

Notice it is the Lord, not the enemy, who caused men to ride over David's head in Psalm 66. This type of persecution was symbolized by the floodwaters in my dream. I was almost overwhelmed by my circumstances—anger and bitterness had set in. And yet, while in the process, I recognized the enemy, repented daily and never stopped praying to have the right responses during my tests. Sometimes I would apologize to my enemy when I missed the mark and operated in the flesh with my responses to persecution. So, I learned to "ride the waves." Although I came out of the floodwaters a little bruised (the enemy even tried to destroy my health through heart palpitations which resulted from sitting for so many hours on the job), He healed me and brought me out into a "wealthy place." I believe the wealth from the golden bed-head not only represents the wealth He is about to entrust us with, but the spiritual wealth we have gained in the wilderness.

The Lord subsequently took me though other floodwaters. I started to get better with my responses to persecution. I learned to look for the enemy and to smile when I saw him coming. I learned that it was not "people" but the enemy using people. For the most part, I kept my focus on "good" thoughts and therefore I was able to withstand most of the persecution. Yet, I still retaliated at times. He would therefore show me sinful areas within myself that needed correction. Folks, I am here to tell the truth and shame the devil. See, the Lord has crucified my flesh in the wilderness, so I come before you humbly, not concerned about what man thinks of me. I know my testimony will help the Body.

The Lord continued this refining until I was able to receive the "fullness" of the apostolic mantle. I cannot say that I am perfect, but I can truly say that I have grown in leaps and bounds over the past few years. Many things that used to faze me simply do not anymore. And still daily the enemy sends temptation our way. We must make a resolve to pass each test. There are some that I have failed, but I never give up. Never quit. The race is not given to the swift, but to those who endure and persevere.

CONCLUSION: NYC GOVERNMENT MOUNTAIN

In conclusion, I again say that I believe the Lord spoke to me in the mantle dream not just for myself personally but for the Body of Christ. The Body corporately has gone through some kind of wilderness stripping and re-molding experience over the past few years. As in the flood dream, some made it and others got washed away (this could represent spiritual or physical death). He has done and is doing a cleansing work in the Body to prepare us for the next move of God. Only a remnant will move forward.

During what I call my "Moses wilderness season," the Lord stationed me in the previously-mentioned legal contract jobs in lower Manhattan, and showed me the blueprint for breakthrough in NYC. Through a series of dreams and divine revelations, He exposed the principalities which must come down. One of those areas is the "Government Mountain." For example, New York recently became one of the states which legalized gay marriages.

Our ministry has been praying over the U.S. and New York City for several years. As an attorney with knowledge of our laws, I have preached passionately for quite some time about being called to tear down principalities affecting the laws of the land and attempting to turn those laws against the Church. Right after a series I taught relating to this issue, the Lord placed our ministry in a NYC public school. What happened next was shocking, but confirmed to me that God had strategically placed me in this area.

In June of 2011, a critical decision came down from the New York Second Circuit (*NYC Department of Education (DOE) v. Bronx Household of Faith*) in violation of the First Amendment rights of the Church. After over 17 years of litigation, the New York appellate court (Second Circuit) upheld the DOE's attempt to evict churches from renting after hours in public schools, although other organizations can rent with no issue. I was previously unaware of this case. As a "legal mind," it is quite evident to me just how discriminatory this holding is. This is a clear violation of the Church's right to religious freedom. Bronx Household lost the case in the first round, but after much prayer, the church re-filed and won in the lower court. The case was heard on appeal before the Second Circuit in November of 2011. A written ruling should be issued in early 2013. We are believing that the appellate court will not reverse this landmark decision.

The Lord, I believe, positioned our ministry in this school – right **after** the negative June ruling and right **before** the re-filing and victory for the Church in the new case. That case had been in limbo for 17 years, with a final decision given immediately before we started renting from the school. There is no coincidence in God. I then realized that He had called me as a forerunner, to come against principalities seeking to destroy our nation in this realm of the Government Mountain. We have had some victories in this case, but the battle is not over. We are hoping that people will continue to stand with us in prayer over this crucial issue that not only affects NY state, but can potentially affect the entire nation.

There are many other revelations the Lord entrusted me with during and after my wilderness season. I can then say to those who question what God has or is doing in their lives, "Be patient; His plans will unfold in time." There has been a "price to pay." He has placed His promises to us on shelves. But, He is about to take the Body of Christ off of the shelf and reveal to the world the true sons of God. We have been anointed for such a time as this. This is a season when the world is about to see the greatest revolution the Church has ever brought forth. He needs each and every one of us to accomplish this.

ABOUT THE AUTHOR

Dr. Michelle A. Morrison is the Senior Apostle of Kingdom Dominion International Ministries, a multi-cultural church located in downtown New York City. Dr. Morrison graduated from Columbia University with a BA in English, and from Georgetown University Law with her Juris Doctorate. She also has earned both Masters and Doctorate degrees in ministry.

Dr. Morrison is a social entrepreneur and the CEO of several organizations, including YesUCan! Community and Economic Development Corporation (YUC!), a social enterprise. The mission of YUC! is to bring financial freedom to the poor cross-culturally. YUC! is a grass-roots organization that seeks to connect the unemployed with job and business resources, as well as to implement other initiatives such as low income housing.

Although a NYC attorney at law, Dr. Morrison advocates primarily the cause of the gospel – the life, death and resurrection of Jesus Christ. She has the fire of Elijah and the warrior call of Deborah to tear down the strongholds of the enemy and re-build the old waste places.

Dr. Morrison is commissioned as a forerunner to "prepare the way of the Lord," and serve as one of the catalysts for the end-time Third Awakening. She is anointed for miracles, signs and wonders, and to fulfill the great commission of spreading the Gospel to the uttermost parts of the earth. To learn more or to contact Dr. Morrison, please visit her websites at www.yesuc.org or www.kingdomdominioninternational.com, email info@kingdomdominioninternational.com, or write to her at PO Box 981, New York, NY 10008-0981.

CHAPTER THIRTY-THREE

THE APOSTOLIC RELEASE

PAUL L. CUNY

THE RIGHT KIND OF LEADER

Jim and I arrived at the retreat center where 30-40 of the leading pastors of our region were gathering for three days of prayer and strategy. We were two of the five marketplace leaders who were invited to join these men and women of God during this prayer meeting. I was like a kid going to his first baseball game. To pray with pastors, men and women of all denominations and ethnic backgrounds for God's move in our region excited me. Jim had attended before and said "Paul, you are going to hear some things, but we just need to stay in the background. Remember to keep your mouth shut; pray and support these guys with our prayer." I said, "No problem! I'm just happy to be with people who pray for serious things."

It was in the late '90s and I was just beginning my apostolic journey. God was beginning to speak to me about being an apostle, but I had no idea what He meant because it did not seem to fit. I had many questions and few answers. "How could a businessman be an apostle?" "Was I really hearing God or was it bad pizza?" "Aren't apostles guys who go around the world planting churches?" "Pastors are apostles, but business people???" There was so little definition at the time. I thought it best to keep this to myself and continue to put it before the Lord. Yet, I was beginning to see things on a much broader scale. God's purpose for my life was beginning to be clarified before my eyes. It is the Lord who enables us to "see" the big picture as He sees it. It is by His grace that this happens, and it is always for His strategic purposes, not for our self-glorification. It is a gift that comes with responsibilities.

In the first session, we were all seated around a huge map of the region taped to the floor. The facilitator said, "When you look at this region, tell me what you see?" One after another of these precious men and women of God, people I had longstanding relationships with, people I had served, contributed to, prayed with and for, began talking about a region I didn't know. Evangelists said people weren't getting saved, pastors said people were leaving the church, youth ministers said young people were not excited about Christ. Some talked about governmental resistance, the lack of finances to do the work of the ministry in the region, and the apparent lack of interest in spiritual things on the part of business leaders. I was surprised by what I was hearing. As they made their way around the circle of leaders, one of these religious leaders said, "We have got to find a way to motivate business leaders to give resources to the vision God has given us for the city."

Suddenly God spoke to me. "Son, they are not talking about the right kind of leader. The kind of leader who will transform this region will not be motivated from their pulpits, because I have motivated them already. I have provided all the resources and leadership needed to accomplish what I have ordained for this region, but they are looking for the wrong kind of leader to do the work.

You don't motivate the kind of leader who will transform; you identify them and release them to do what I have called them to do." Without thinking, I jumped out of my seat and repeated what God had just said. My comments were followed by this uncomfortably long period of silence. Finally, the facilitator said, "Brother, you are not a pastor, are you?" One of the leading pastors pointed his finger at me, smiled, and nodded his head approvingly. He understood.

MOTIVATION TO TRANSFORM

The city of Jerusalem was in a shambles. The people were heavily taxed; they were being slaughtered by their oppressors. Their children were being taken and sold into slavery, families were being torn apart and there was no protection for the remnant left in Jerusalem. While all this was taking place, Ezra, the renowned priest, scholar and writer of a book of the Bible, was holding temple services for over 14 years. Then, 900 miles away, God "motivated" one of His leaders to produce transformation. God was not random in His timing or His priorities in this model of transformation.

First, He sent Ezra the priest, and then 14 years later He sent Nehemiah. Nehemiah was not motivated to lead the re-building of the wall of Jerusalem from going to temple and listening to the Rabbi's Sabbath message. God identified this man, offered him the opportunity to share in this strategic moment in history, and with no apparent resume to indicate his capability, Nehemiah accepted the offer. After he arrived in the ruins of Jerusalem, Nehemiah revealed something that is telling in Neh. 2:16: *"The officials did not know where I had gone or what I had done; nor had I as yet told the Jews, the priests, the nobles, the officials or the rest who did the work."*

The apostolic emergence we are all seeing is a move of God that He will continue to define for us in the coming generations. It is not going away. It is a move of anointed, empowered, sovereignly-appointed leaders who operate with all the Biblical mandates to produce Kingdom change. Change of any nature has rarely been embraced by established structures, whether they are commercial, governmental or religious structures. My observation is that many apostolic religious leaders seem to struggle with the understanding and recognition of apostles to the marketplace. I was talking with an 82-year old apostle to apostles recently who has written the most scholarly work on apostles I have read to date.[1] "If you would have told me even five years ago that there were apostles in the marketplace," he said, "I would have considered it heresy. However, I now understand that this must be the case."

APOSTLES TO THE MARKETPLACE

Apostles to the marketplace (apostles in government and commerce) are beginning to be acknowledged and released in ways we have not seen before. Most moves of God begin with the apologist who goes to the existing religious establishment and says, "What is happening is a move of God and it is legitimate." Then the activation phase begins the release of the effects of God's hand in this move. I believe we have entered the activation phase. This usually comes with some resistance because it is new and often viewed as a challenge to the status quo. Yet, it is through these apostles in the marketplace that God will create the conditions in their respective nations for the church to flourish. They are the leaders who carry the anointing and power to establish His Kingdom influence in government or in commerce.

Most apostles to the marketplace do not have a pulpit to speak to thousands every week, yet they are lovers of the church in all of its expressions, whether that expression is a home church or a mega church, because those expressions represent the Bride of Christ. Most books I have read over the years on the apostolic are written by ministry leaders who have these pulpits of the world. In these books, there is usually a paragraph or two that says something like, "We believe there are apostles in the marketplace; we think this is what they look like, but they are largely hidden and we will understand them more in the days ahead."

Certainly, more definition is necessary, but this ambiguity is clearly one of the unintended consequences of the sacred/secular mindset. Just like the prayer meeting I spoke of above, the very people God sends to cities and nations to exercise His influence over governments or commerce often are ignored by the Western church, or considered second tier in spiritual authority or anointing, rather than being embraced and released. When we ignore God's gift to nations, the church creates a leadership vacuum in the positions of power and influence in cities and nations that the enemy quickly fills. As we all grow in our understanding, and recognize and release this critical segment of apostolic leadership in business and government, we will finally begin to see the change in culture that so many religious and marketplace leaders are crying out for all over the world.

My observation is that apostles in the marketplace, by and large, have not stepped into the fullness of this calling yet. This is a general observation and I don't want to be dogmatic about this statement. Some are walking in all the authority God has given them, but I believe that most are not. Some of this is the timing of the Lord, as He brings us much-needed understanding and definition, and some is spiritual maturity, character development, and personal growth. It is our hope that this book provides some of that definition and understanding.

TEN OBSERVATIONS ABOUT APOSTOLIC LEADERSHIP

I would like to offer some of my observations about apostolic leadership in the marketplace to perhaps provide a further definition and release to these unique leaders.

1. **Apostles are born apostles.** Whether they oversee 100 churches or are CEO of a Fortune 500 company (Ps. 139:13), they were born with "apostle" as their destiny. Apostles are not promoted to the position by a particular achievement in their sphere. They do not "achieve" apostleship by being successful in business or government. In God's sovereignty, He appoints; we don't achieve. Making lots of money isn't the qualification for the calling of an apostle in the same way that pastoring a mega church doesn't make you an apostle. It is a direct call from God, just like a call to the ministry of the evangelist or pastor.

   The apostle Paul, to his contemporaries, had none of the trappings of what the modern religious world would deem requirements for apostleship. He was publically beaten, shipwrecked, and stoned, worked as a tentmaker, and wasn't very "attractive." Most of us would have thought, "The guy needs to get another job, because this one will kill him – no favor!" Yet, Paul understood he was appointed by God and exercised all the authority that came with that appointment.

2. **Most apostles to the marketplace are very quiet about their calling.** There are several reasons for this silence, but the primary reason I have seen is intimidation. There is the intimidation from a religious world that does not understand or acknowledge this kind of apostle. There is intimidation from the enemy to hinder what God wants to do through you, and there is intimidation because you just don't believe God's choice. An apostle friend of mine gave me a release I needed in this area when he told me one time, "Your responsibility is to recognize God's choice without apology, even if you are His choice."

3. **Apostles to the marketplace often under-utilize the authority they have been given.** Authentic authority is delegated to you by God to produce change, signs, and wonders in your particular sphere. You are to exercise that authority seven days a week – signs and wonders in the board room, signs and wonders over manufacturing equipment and business deals and projects, etc. Signs and wonders follow apostles to the marketplace – it needs to be our normal lifestyle.

4. **Apostles to the marketplace are ambassadors who represent the government of the Kingdom of God and its Sovereign Ruler in their sphere.** As ambassadors, you represent the interests of your Leader and Government and not your own. I have several close friends who are ambassadors and they constantly say, "My President believes..." or "The position of my government is..." Ambassadors speak

FOR their King, not themselves. If you are always trying to represent your own interests, increase your visibility, and/or demand personal recognition, you are not worthy of representing your King. If you make a mistake, or you overstep your bounds, don't be paralyzed into inactivity. The Lord will gently correct you so you won't make that mistake again. He trusts His ambassadors. Don't be timid.

5. **Apostles to the marketplace are fully provisioned to carry out their assignment when the assignment meets the timing of God.** Apostles usually carry specific assignments. Just as an ambassador of a nation is not concerned about how to pay for his plane ticket on government business, neither should you concern yourself about these things when you are on Government business. Focus on your assignment and God's timing and the provision will be waiting for you.

6. **Apostles to the marketplace seem to be frustrated by the lack of affirmation from the religious leadership.** I have heard this frustration expressed in many different ways by many prominent leaders. Coupled with this calling you have, will eventually come the recognition by others with a similar calling (Acts 13:1-4). The apostle Paul was recognized by the other apostles that he was indeed one of them. Paul's pastor or Rabbi may not have "affirmed" him, but the other apostles did. You are responsible before God to fulfill your assignment. No one on earth is keeping you from walking in your calling, so don't use "affirmation" as an excuse for not doing what you are born, created and designed to do. Walk in your calling.

7. **Apostles to the marketplace will have a fathering heart to their leadership** (1 Cor. 4:15). It doesn't matter whether you are in the religious world or the marketplace; this is a characteristic of all apostolic leadership. It is the expression of the Father's heart toward those they lead, whether it is a business or government leadership; the Father's heart is always expressed by providing godly leadership, counsel, and common sense to life issues that are confirmed by Scripture. Isa. 22:21 describes a man named Eliakim, who was about to be "appointed" by God to a high position of governmental leadership.

At the same time God was announcing Eliakim's appointment, He was announcing that He was removing the wicked man who was in that position. In speaking of Eliakim, He said, *"I will entrust him with your authority, And he will become a father to the inhabitants of Jerusalem and to the house of Judah."* Fathers don't dominate or denigrate sons; they don't demand tribute from sons, or sell their fatherhood for a price. Fathers encourage and help foster the gifts and callings of their sons and daughters. A father's chief joy is to see his sons walk securely with God and in their God-given gifts.

8. **Apostles in the marketplace must live a sanctified life before God.** One of the Greek definitions for "sanctify" is "to separate from profane things, to dedicate to God, to consecrate or so render inviolable."[2] The sacred/secular mindset will tell you that only those in "full-time ministry" are required to live in holiness, but this deception will keep you from walking through life in its fullness. Life as an apostle

requires a life of consecration. Whether you preach on Sunday morning, or lead a board meeting on Monday morning, the requirement is the same. You don't accept bribes; you don't engage in questionable business practices because you carry the presence of God as His ambassador, and you do nothing to violate that high honor or office. You bring context to the culture of your area of authority rather than allowing the culture to influence you and others you lead.

9. **Apostles in the marketplace have a keen sense of God's authority system.** There must be recognition of the priesthood and their role in the Body of Christ, whether you are recognized by the priesthood or not. The work God will do through you in the days ahead will not be accomplished by apostolic marketplace leaders alone, or by ecclesiastical ministry leaders alone, but rather in cooperation with one another. The King of Persia sent the first group of exiles back to Jerusalem to rebuild the Temple. He sent two men to lead this group of exiles, Joshua the High Priest (tribe of Levi) and Zerubbabel the Governor (tribe of Judah). In Zechariah Chapter 4, God shows the prophet two olive trees beside the lampstand, through which oil flows. He then describes how he sees the priest and the government leader in verse 14, *"These are the two anointed ones who are standing by the Lord of the whole earth."*

Properly translated, "two anointed ones" means "sons of oil." They each had different roles to bring God's order to the culture of their day, but the same oil flowed through both of them. Zerubbabel was essential to create the governmental order and structure for Joshua's ministry to flourish. The same is true today. Whether your pastor, minister, reverend, bishop or apostle embraces your calling or not, your responsibilities before God do not change. Yet, you are required to honor the priesthood in thought, word and deed, while you walk out your calling. Proper alignment by the Spirit with leadership of small groups, your church, ministry, synagogue or fellowship is an important element of this kind of leadership.

10. **Apostles in the marketplace have a passion to know God and His ways.** You must be students of Scripture, people of prayer, and above all have a consuming desire to be a friend of God. Personal intimacy with God and times of communion are essential; these are elements in the lives of everyone who will represent the King in any capacity and they are not optional for you. The strategies for change will come; your abilities and giftings will be utilized, but your highest calling is to be God's friend.

We are all walking in unfamiliar territory, but the Apostolic Reformation that is taking place is a work of God and He is defining the various facets of it for us through revelation and Scripture on a daily basis. You and I are in what I believe is the greatest season of history. The systems of commerce and government are waiting for your release. You were created to live an extraordinary life and define these important spheres of culture, rather than be defined by them. You are released to live out your role in this cultural definition to the fullest.

ENDNOTES

1. Ernest Gentile, *Why Apostles Now?*, Moses Lake, WA: BT Johnson Publishing, 2011.
2. Thayer's Greek Lexicon, Electronic Database. Copyright © 2000 by Biblesoft.

ABOUT THE AUTHOR

Paul Cuny is President of MarketPlace Leadership International, an organization dedicated to bringing the Biblical realities of the Kingdom to the marketplace. Paul's background as an entrepreneur, investor, and business owner has given him a unique platform from which to speak to leaders and professionals. He is an ordained minister with the apostolic and prophetic assignment to "… change the economies of nations."

Paul has taught Kingdom principles of Kingdom business and leadership throughout Africa, South America, Central America and the U.S. He is an international conference and church speaker on the Kingdom Economy and Kingdom Leadership. Paul has been interviewed on international TV and radio on the restoration of the economy of the Kingdom that is taking place. He is a prolific writer and the author of the book *Secrets of the Kingdom Economy* which is published in English and Portuguese. He has spoken on international TV and radio. He has served as a friend, counselor and prayer partner to sitting presidents, ambassadors, business and government leaders around the world. You can find more information about Paul at his website, www.marketplaceleadership.com.

CHAPTER THIRTY-FOUR

BECOMING APOSTLES OF MERIT

DR. PHILIP R. BYLER

As I write this, the term "emerging apostle" receives a considerable amount of use. This term accompanies the much wider vocabulary recently developed. The term "apostle of merit" allows us to identify those who, empowered with significant authority and responsibility, have demonstrated exceptional faithfulness. These men and women have earned the right to be recognized as leaders of leaders. Among the ranks of the apostolic community, they are more highly honored and esteemed.

Scripture admonishes us to render honor where honor is due (Rom. 13:7), and that certain elders are worthy of double honor (1 Tim. 5:17). Apostleship alone does not project the level of honor that some of our apostolic brothers and sisters merit. There is more.

What sets them apart? What makes them worthy of honor more than others who carry the title and responsibility of apostle? There are certainly many factors one should consider, but I believe there are three that stand out above other factors. Of course, every apostle should demonstrate these perspectives in their lives. But apostles of merit have done it so well, and for so long, that those who follow their lead recognize them above their peers.

THEY ARE EXEMPLARY MODELS

The first characteristic I would suggest that brings such recognition is the excellence of their example. Apostles of merit are men and women whose character, achievements, faithfulness, and longevity are models to the whole apostolic community. Their lives demonstrate the highest level of apostolic presence. This presence lends power to their message and prestige to their position. Their lives are visible examples of the message they preach and provide a clearly-defined pattern for others to follow. This is extremely important, especially in a time when we are inundated with people of lesser stature, seeking to be recognized throughout the Christian community.

We have seen many Christian leaders, after attaining levels of celebrity and status that caused them to be honored among men, fall. When they did, not only was their character tarnished, but their failures cast a shadow of guilt by association across the church overall. We loudly· proclaim that the fall of one does not reflect on the rest. We know that is not completely true. We are all in this together. When one suffers, we all suffer (1 Cor. 12:26).

Apostles of merit model a life of devotion and dedication to Jesus and to His Kingdom. They demonstrate their commitment by action. They are unafraid of examination or public scrutiny because they have little or nothing to hide. Interestingly, if they do hide their flaws, God has a way of revealing their failures, first to themselves, then to their covering. This is not to expose them to public ridicule or condemnation. Rather, it is to provide them opportunity to correct those issues.

If in turn they refuse correction or adjustment from their covering, He eventually will expose them to the general public. Men will "shout it from the housetops" (Luke 12:3) and God will "let the chips fall where they may." Those who will not humble themselves, God will humble. And the only way He can humble an individual is to let him or her face humiliation. Never think that someone has no areas that need correction simply because others have been exposed. Apart from the grace of God, we all would find ourselves in similar positions of exposure and shame. Achieving longevity as an apostle is, in many ways, a living testimony to an individual's willingness to keep short accounts with God. Such leaders are quick to repent in times of weakness and are utterly determined to walk worthy of the calling wherewith they are called.

Those who will not humble themselves, God will humble.

Apostolic leaders must elevate their own example to the highest level of excellence so that others will copy only the best in their lives, not the worst. When people see that an example is commendable and credible, they copy it. They pattern their lives and ministries after the one they see, elevating the level of prestige an apostle carries, and increasing the power of his or her voice.

THEY ROUTINELY HONOR OTHER PEOPLE

The second reason to acknowledge apostles of merit is their consistent determination to give honor to others. Giving honor preserves apostolic integrity. Honor is the determination to bestow upon another person a level of esteem and significance greater than your own. It is of no concern that others may esteem you more highly than the person you are honoring. Giving honor is the act of giving respect to the very personhood and God-given worth of people. It resides high on the list of apostolic priorities, and demonstrates a self-imposed humility that both enables and takes delight in the success of others.

Giving honor preserves apostolic integrity.

Apostles of merit consistently defend the honor of others. They refuse to embrace and readily address as unacceptable that which is dishonorable. Actions or communications that are degrading, demeaning, or detrimental to the reputation, character, or personhood of those they esteem are quickly and uncompromisingly rebuffed. In so doing, these apostolic leaders provide a safe haven for redemption and restoration while ever promoting an environment of transformation.

Apostles of merit also communicate their honor of others, and that not merely in lip service. They understand and live their lives aware that honor is not measured by what is spoken. Honor is measured by how well the life and living of the one honored is protected and advanced. They refuse to bow to a lesser standard through convenience or apparent necessity and show themselves to be persons of honor through their consistently honorable behavior.

THEY CULTIVATE BENEFICIAL HABITS

I propose yet a third evidence of why a person should be recognized as an apostle of merit. That is their habits. Habits tend to reveal our most basic character qualities as well as our weaknesses and flaws.

Everyone has habits—some are good, some are bad. Habits hold significance because that which is habit becomes ingrained in character. Habits determine how people will manage their affairs. Habits determine how people will respond to people, embracing some and resisting others. Habits determine how people will respond in times of trial, temptation, or crisis. Truly our habits have a great impact on life and ministry.

An old proverb states this fact quite well:

Sow a thought, reap an action—Sow an action, reap a habit—
Sow a habit, reap your character—
Sow your character, reap your destiny.
—Samuel Smiles

Apostles of merit demonstrate a high level of attention to good habits as opposed to bad ones. They routinely honor people. They treat people with dignity. They show generosity and kindness, and in a hundred other ways, they demonstrate lives filled with beneficial routines. These shape their character and make them attractive to people. This gives them voice—the ability to speak and be heard—and causes people to hold them in high esteem. Such habits project a persona that people respond to well. It causes them to better appreciate the input these people have into their lives.

Unfortunately, there are other things in our lives that we seldom pay attention to. We routinely act in ways that are highly repetitive. These activities are so "daily" we pay them little mind. Yet, we should all be conscious that we need to minimize our bad habits and maximize our good ones.

NEGLECT HARMS THE ANOINTING

Problem habits are things like habitual neglect, carelessness, overeating, and self-centeredness. We can add disobedience to God, negativity, tardiness, rudeness, arrogance, crude speech, laziness, and slovenly appearance, and a whole lot more. Habits like these could be defeated with relative ease by a strong dose of self-imposed discipline. But, we can only defeat them if we pay attention to them and challenge their existence in our lives.

I find that not breaking my bad habits is primarily a result of not paying attention to them. I tend to notice them only at those times when they are called to my attention. Sometimes I purposely give them a glance. All too often I pay them no heed. Thus, they have a tendency to control my methods and manners far more than I would really like to admit. But, not all of my habits are bad, and neither are yours.

We can build constructive habits, but not through neglect—which itself is a bad habit. Good habits cause us to effectively extend the reach of our influence and authority. Habits like obedience to God, generosity, prayer, and a positive outlook are extremely beneficial. Honoring others requires us to be attentive to others. Good manners and respectable behavior, humility and careful speech, punctuality and kindness, and a host of other good qualities are the stuff that causes people to enjoy hanging around us.

Most people are not simply looking for the next revelation that drips from the lips of the sage pilgrim. They are also looking for likable, loveable, and enjoyable people who care about them and desire to see them grow strong.

Apostles of merit have mastered these things and habitually make people comfortable and secure. Such quality habits establish a person's persona. They are attractive and they attract people.

THE PROTECTION OF PERSONA

The protection of persona is also tremendously important. It is important to you, and it is important to every other member of the body of Christ. Whenever a Christian fails to live up to the expectations of his persona, when he or she fails to uphold the highest standards of behavior—seen or unseen, the resulting response is predictable and is seldom good. None of us lives unto himself. We live unto the Lord and we live in connectivity with every other believer. Apostles of merit carefully and with great wisdom protect their persona so that others will not stumble over their weaknesses.

With every elevation in role or responsibility, there is a corresponding elevation in the need to protect one's good name. *"A good name is to be chosen rather than great riches"* (Prov. 22:1a). That good name must reflect the quality of character it projects.

None of us lives unto himself. We live unto the Lord and we live in connectivity with every other believer.

There are many levels of authority and responsibility in the church. Apostles are entrusted with the highest levels. But, they do not all carry comparable levels of authority. And they certainly do not all have comparable responsibilities. Considerable differences in the nature, size, and impact of various apostolic spheres are readily apparent. Still, there is no more responsible calling than that of apostle. The apostle is to be an exemplar—a living example of Kingdom experience and ministry. This is just as true for each of the five-fold ministries and for the offices of the nuclear church—the organized body of believers.

Christians do not lose their humanity when they experience salvation. They continue to respond to very human emotions, perspectives, and preferences. We have an affinity for heroes. We like winners. We are easily drawn to believe that what others have, we can have also. This is especially true in the United States where Christianity is on open display.

Highly visible ministerial personalities portray a kind of Christianity that is seldom available to ordinary people—people who live their lives outside of the bubble of celebrity. We are easily convinced that the persona we see on the screen (or the platform) is the same as the one that is lived off-screen. It may well be, and unless otherwise indicated, we tend to believe it is. But, we never know for certain whether it is or not. That is, not unless something occurs that exposes error or tarnishes their image. Then everyone knows.

Because most people are not in the position to know the intimacies or intricacies of an apostle's life, they tend to believe that the apostolic leader is somehow "better." Perhaps he or she is more spiritual, or more skilled, or more prosperous, or healthier. Breaches in exemplary behavior and violations of moral excellence are often covered up so that the general public does not see. Even when such missteps are exposed, people are quick to overlook such flaws, because they are enjoined not to judge. *"Judge not, that you be not judged"* (Matt. 7:1) is often the biblical admonition used to disallow honest evaluation of any corrective or restoration process.

We need to dig deeper here. There is a biblical proposition that is quite opposite from that. At first reading, we easily see that we are told not to judge. But, reading further, and maintaining the context of the injunction, we are told something else. We are told that the standard of judgment we project upon others will be used against us. In truth, we are actually instructed to judge—only to judge with righteous judgment. *"Do not judge according to appearance, but judge with righteous judgment"* (John 7:24). That is a bit more difficult.

Here is the problem. We often apply unrighteous judgment—judgment that is either too harsh or too weak. It is all too easy to apply judgment that is legalistic and fail to look at our own frailty. It is just as easy to try to smoothe over something that truly needs correction. We choose not to judge. We choose to ignore the obvious and accept the status quo. Unfortunately, our reluctance to render judgment has allowed more than a few impostors and pretenders to slip through the cracks. Becoming an apostle is no shallow responsibility. No one should attempt to become one without understanding the demanding lifestyle that must accompany the office.

Apostles are vulnerable to character weaknesses just like everyone else. But, in apostles, those character flaws are quickly and ruthlessly exploited. So, when reaching for a mantle of apostolic responsibility, people need to exercise extreme caution. If an individual intends to succeed in the apostolic, he or she must be single-minded in their effort to live at the highest level of godliness, holiness, and moral excellence. Their word must be their bond. Everyone must be able to trust them... trust their judgment... trust their wisdom... and trust the integrity of their relationship with God. Over time, such reliable men and women will become apostles of merit, and the whole body of Christ will be blessed by their lives.

Editor's Note: This chapter was originally included as part of *Profiles in Protocol* by Dr. Philip R. Byler, which was published in 2008 by Palm Tree Productions and is used by permission of the author. Unless otherwise noted, scripture references and citations are taken from the New King James Version of the Bible.)

ABOUT THE AUTHOR

Dr. Philip R. Byler is a seasoned writer and speaker—a pioneer in the apostolic movement who has taken the Kingdom message around the world. He is the founder and director of C.T.T.M. Ministries International. Dedicated to assisting churches and church leaders transition into apostolic life, his message is firmly set against a separation between the sacred and the secular. Philip brings the unique perspective of an insider to the development of effective ministry beyond the boundaries of church infrastructure and to the expanding workplace ministry movement.

Dr. Byler is also an author and a ghost writer, working under the brand The Phantom Scribe. His company, PB&J Designs, offers a variety of services including graphic design services for businesses and ministries, book layout for publishing, writing skills development, coaching and mentoring for writers, and writing workshops. Dr. Byler and his wife, Dr. Judy Byler, reside in the mountains of North Georgia. To learn more or contact him, visit his website at www.philipbyler.com.

CHAPTER THIRTY-FIVE

RECOGNIZING APOSTLES

ROBERT HENDERSON

As we have moved forward in our efforts to bring reformation within nations, it has become clear this cannot happen without the apostolic and in particular without apostles. I believe that much of what we have sought to accomplish was impossible in times gone by because apostles were yet to be in place. The apostolic's proper placement has required and continues to require a restoration process. It is a common understanding now, that the restoration process has been in a reverse order in which the five-fold ministry gifts were first mentioned. In Eph. 4:11, we see the apostle Paul listing the ministry gifts that would be used to fashion the church. The church or the ecclesia (God's governing people) is absolutely necessary if we are to see society reformed and nations discipled.

"And He Himself gave some to be apostles, some prophets, some evangelists, and some pastors and teachers."

The restoration process began in the '50s and '60s and saw the gift of Pastor restored. During this period we saw people discovering the grace of God upon their life to care for others in the body of Christ and help them overcome their history and discover their Kingdom destiny.

The next gift that was restored in the '70s was the teacher gift. I grew up to a large degree during this time. I remember church services, home Bible studies, prayer gatherings and other events with teaching being the center point of these times. People would show up with their tape recorders, Bibles, notebooks and multicolor pens to underline the revelation these teachers were unveiling. During this time, the charismatic movement was underway. We witnessed a return to the manifestations or gifts of the Holy Spirit as these teachers unveiled for us the principles and powers of the Godhead.

In the '70s and '80s we began to see the evangelist gift functioning. Not only was there a declaration of the saving grace of the Lord Jesus Christ, but this message began to be accompanied with signs and wonders. This continues to develop even until this day as the church matures into the function of the power gifts that will convince the lost of who Jesus really is.

The next gift that was restored was prophet. This began to be restored in the '80s and '90s. Men and women began to speak forth the counsels of the Lord. We continue to see the prophetic ministry develop and learn to function with the apostolic today. This is essential in that the foundation of the church is the apostles and prophets. Eph. 2:20 tells us that the church/ecclesia will be rooted in the apostolic and prophetic ministry.

"...having been built on the foundation of the apostles and prophets, Jesus Christ Himself being the chief cornerstone."

Apostles and prophets functioning together release a dynamic power that establishes the Kingdom rule in spheres of society. We cannot see this occur without both of these ministries. Apostles need the revelation of the prophets but prophets need the strategy and authority of the apostles. When these two gifts function together, we see heaven invade the earth and Kingdom order begins to be seen.

THE RESTORATION OF THE APOSTLE GIFT

Apostles began to be re-established around 2001. Dr. C. Peter Wagner states that the Second Apostolic Age began then from his research in this season. This is not to say that there were no apostles before then. It is just to say that the apostolic movement came to a new realm. It seems that the Lord began to deal with people who have this gift and cause them to accept this calling. Most of these apostles who began to emerge and function were slow to accept this title. This is because the real apostles are not power hungry and are not quick to claim authority. They actually are very humble people who see the authority granted them is to be wielded with great surrender and in the fear of the Lord.

In the midst of the restoration of the apostolic gift, we need to be able to recognize what apostles are. I know that this may seem elementary given the fact we are many years down the road in this present apostolic movement. Yet, I find that there is still a great amount of confusion about who an apostle is and what they do. Therefore, I want to give several characteristics of an apostle.

Apostles first and foremost carry a realm of authority that is necessary to establish kingdom rule. Paul spoke of the authority that he had from the Lord. 2 Cor. 10:8 tells us what the authority Paul had been granted was for.

"For even if I should boast somewhat more about our authority, which the Lord gave us for edification and not for your destruction, I shall not be ashamed."

The authority that an apostle carries is always to build up and not tear down. Out of this authority, the other characteristics of an apostle are manifest.

From an apostle's authority, they deal with principalities that resist the kingdom of God in the earth. Eph. 6:12 tells us that Paul wrestled with this demonic hierarchy to see regions freed and people groups able to accept the Lord. Marketplace apostles definitely need to see this happen. We are of the conviction that without the shifting of the spirit realm, there can be no success or reformation in the natural realm.

"For we do not wrestle against flesh and blood, but against principalities, against powers, against the rulers of the darkness of this age, against spiritual hosts of wickedness in the heavenly places."

One of the reasons we have not been tremendously successful in undoing this devilish hierarchy is because we haven't had apostles in a mature state. As apostles grow in their authority, these demonic powers will be neutralized and dismantled. When this happens, the hearts of men will be freed to come to kingdom perspectives. Multitudes will be saved because that which has blinded their hearts has vanished. Society will begin to take on the "shape" of that which is now ruling the atmosphere and not the previous principalities and powers.

As a result of the authority that apostles carry, once powers of darkness are wrestled into submission, there is also a grace of a wise master builder that is operated in. In 1 Cor. 3:10, Paul claims a grace that allowed him to build that which was permanent.

"According to the grace of God which was given to me, as a wise master builder I have laid the foundation, and another builds on it. But let each one take heed how he builds on it."

APOSTLES ARE BUILDERS

Apostles have plans and strategies that allow them to build according to the pattern of heaven. Real apostles are builders at their very core. Whether they are building local churches, apostolic networks, schools, businesses or other entities for the kingdom of God, there is a physical demonstration of the authority that they carry. What they build testifies to the apostolic grace in their lives. This is what Paul spoke of in 1 Cor. 9:1-2.

"Am I not an apostle? Am I not free? Have I not seen Jesus Christ our Lord? Are you not my work in the Lord? If I am not an apostle to others, yet doubtless I am to you. For you are the seal of my apostleship in the Lord."

Paul told the Corinthians that they verified the apostolic authority he walked in. The fact that they existed as a church said he was an apostle. Apostles always have something they can point to that they have built. This is a result of the authority they carry.

From the authority they carry, apostles function in the miraculous. In 2 Cor. 12:12, Paul says that signs and wonders are the sign of apostles.

"Truly the signs of an apostle were accomplished among you with all perseverance, in signs and wonders and mighty deeds."

We see this in the early church when the apostles performed healings and miracles. The difference between signs and wonders of an apostle and signs and wonders from one of the other ministry gifts is the source from which they are performed. Apostles perform signs and wonders as an extension of the authority they carry while others see signs and wonders from the anointing or gift in their lives. There is a difference between authority and anointing. Anointing is gift based while authority is born out of revelation. I don't want to make too big of an issue here, but when apostles function from the grace on their lives, atmospheres change. Acts 2:43 shows that the miracles that were happening from apostolic authority came as a result of a shifting of atmosphere.

"Then fear came upon every soul, and many wonders and signs were done through the apostles."

As the fear of the Lord was upon them, which produced the right atmosphere, signs and wonders were done. Authority shifts atmospheres. As the apostles released who they were in God, spiritual forces that challenged the kingdom of God were moved out and a holy fear of the Lord was established. The result was an atmosphere that allowed "many" wonders and signs to be done. The word "many" means so much that it is common. When apostles from their authority adjust the atmosphere, signs and wonders multiply and even become a common thing. The anointing may get a few miracles, but the authority invested in apostles creates an atmosphere that allows a wholesale release of miracles. In the marketplace when apostles carry this authority, they see atmospheres adjusted, which is conducive to success and blessing.

Another realm of the authority that apostles carry is perseverance. 2 Cor. 12:12 lists perseverance as one of the signs of an apostle.

"Truly the signs of an apostle were accomplished among you with all perseverance, in signs and wonders and mighty deeds."

Paul understood that if he kept releasing the authority he carried in God and did not become discouraged or distracted, he would move powers of darkness out and away. Apostles that understand the authority they carry know that if they keep pushing they will win. The devil's only hope is to discourage the heart of the apostles so they quit. If the apostles persevere in their efforts and God-ordained assignments, there will be a whittling away at demonic strongholds until they fall. In the process of perseverance, God unveils strategies to apostles so they with great wisdom can undo whatever resists Kingdom purposes.

Apostles do not approach assignments from the Lord with a temporary mindset. They know that their engagement of the enemy as they seek to take away (dispossess) territory he has controlled, will require length of time normally. They therefore set their face like steel to see God's will done and will willingly lay their lives down for this purpose.

APOSTLES UNVEIL AND STEWARD MYSTERIES

In 1 Cor. 4:1-2, Paul spoke of himself and those with him as stewards of the mysteries of God.

"Let a man so consider us, as servants of Christ and stewards of the mysteries of God. Moreover, it is required in stewards that one be found faithful."

Apostles steward and administrate mysteries from God. There are truths that have been held uncovered since before the foundation of the earth. God unveils these secrets and mysteries to apostles so they can deposit them into the ecclesia. There is nothing as powerful in the earth as revelation. Revelation received has the power to change the way we think and then function. Revelation brings breakthrough that, before it was received, nothing seemed to move the resistant thing. God uses apostles to unveil these mysteries. This is actually where the authority that an apostle has comes from. Authority is the result of revelation. Paul experienced this. In Gal. 1:15-16, Paul shares where he got his authority from that allowed him to shake cities and nations.

"But when it pleased God, who separated me from my mother's womb and called me through His grace, to reveal His Son in me, that I might preach Him among the Gentiles, I did not immediately confer with flesh and blood."

Notice that it was the revealing of His Son that Paul preached and ministered from. Paul was not regurgitating what someone else had said about Jesus and His kingdom. He was speaking mysteries from the revelation of the Lord. As he did, the Gentile world was altered and changed.

We must have real apostles that carry real authority because they have been entrusted with mysteries of the kingdom. When these mysteries are revealed, the power contained in them will alter the church and then society.

There are many things associated with the mysteries that apostles steward. I want to address just one. Col. 1:25-26 gives us insight into part of the nature of mysteries that apostles steward.

"...of which I became a minister according to the stewardship from God which was given to me for you, to fulfill the word of God, the mystery which has been hidden from ages and from generations, but now has been revealed to His saints."

Here again Paul speaks of the stewardship he has toward the mysteries of God. Notice that this mystery was hidden from ages and generations, but had a revealing point. This means that apostles are given insight into things that haven't been seen or heard before. They were hidden from previous ages so that they could be unfolded to the church now. The church of history didn't need these mysteries, but the one now does. It is the unfolding of these mysteries that will propel the church into its glory that is necessary for this time, age and season.

It is apostles who are given the stewardship of these mysteries to unlock them for this dispensation. Don't let the term "dispensation" alarm you. It simply means that which God intends to "dispense" in this time. Without these mysteries being unlocked and dispensed, the church will be stuck where it is and unable to accomplish what is needful for now. The revealed truth to the church in past times is not sufficient for what God will use the church for today. We must have the truth and mysteries reserved for today brought to us by apostles commissioned of God to steward them.

The sad fact is that the church so often is stuck in its traditions. We think we already know everything, so when mysteries start to be unveiled, we are resistant. We actually resist the very unveiling of mysteries that have the power to produce a new authority that the satanic forces can't overwhelm. This is what made the church so powerful in the beginning. They continued and walked in the "apostles' doctrine." In Acts 2:42, the church is drinking deeply of the revelation that the apostles were releasing.

"And they continued steadfastly in the apostles' doctrine and fellowship, in the breaking of bread, and in prayers."

Among other things they continued in, the first thing mentioned was the apostles' doctrine. This was not some dry teaching. This was mysteries the apostles were depositing into this new ecclesia that caused it to be unstoppable. It was what they needed for the season and time they lived in. We also need the mysteries shown to us by the apostles in this hour. We need the dispensing of what is appointed for this dispensation of the church. It will come through the apostles because they are the ones who are commissioned of God to steward these mysteries. May the Lord continue to raise up recognizable apostles who are growing in their authority and maturity until the church in every sphere is what we were meant to be. Apostles come with the mysteries of God and impregnate the church with them until we function as God's ecclesia.

ABOUT THE AUTHOR

With a passion to see the Lord's kingdom come to earth in a tangible way, Robert Henderson is a man of undistracted devotion. Whether it is through the apostolic teaching gift that he has been given, the demonstration of signs and wonders or the governmental authority that flows from the Throne of God, Robert desires to see God's kingdom come to earth and Jesus' will being done.

Robert is the apostolic overseer of Global Reformers network, and senior pastor of WellSprings Church, and the director of Robert Henderson Ministries. Robert and his wife Mary have been married and in full-time ministry for over 30 years, and have six children and three grandchildren. Robert is a prolific author, eloquent speaker and dynamic minister, and has published several volumes of apostolic revelation for the church, marketplace and Kingdom, including *The Caused Blessing: Connecting to Apostolic Power through Strategic Giving, Consecrated Business: Apostolically Aligning the Marketplace, The Secret of the Lord: Direction for Life through Intimacy with Him, Apostolic Dominion through Signs and Wonders,* and *A Voice of Reformation: An Apostolic and Prophetic View of Each of the Seven Mountains in a Reformed State.*

Robert has also been awarded an honorary doctorate for life experience by North Carolina College of Theology. You may learn more about his ministry or contact him through the following websites: www.globalreformers.com or www.wellspringschurchcs.org or www.roberthenderson.org.

CHAPTER THIRTY-SIX

THE SIGNS OF APOSTLESHIP

LLOYD PHILLIPS

CHARACTER COMES FIRST

How do we know who is truly called of God to apostolic ministry? What about false apostles and false prophets? There has been a significant amount of discussion on judging ministries for oneself and I have had significant experience and time to give serious consideration and reflection to this subject. What I have learned may be of help in discerning true, false, functioning, fallen, or those immature in ministry. These are my thoughts, based upon study of the scripture and application though my experiences. This study, to the best of my ability, has been rightly divided in light of my scope and understanding of scripture, limited though it may be, including some practical application in light of the ministry of apostleship.

In 2 Cor. 12:12 (KJV) the apostle Paul wrote what he called the signs of an apostle, *"Truly the signs of an apostle were wrought among you in all patience, in signs, and wonders, and mighty deeds."* Paul is clearly speaking of his apostleship in this verse, and in the immediate context of this verse. He was not defending his Christianity as no one questioned that he was a Christian, not even Nero when he was later brought before him. However, men had come into Corinth and had caused the church there to question his apostolic ministry, which he was here defending.

The vast majority of people reading this verse believe Paul is stating that the signs of his apostleship were signs, wonders and miracles. In my own characterization of apostles and the apostolic movement, I have never made excuses to those who want to see more signs and wonders. An old apostle once told me that we should keep a file of the miracles God has done through our ministry or for us just to go through from time to time for encouragement and faith building.

It's not for anyone else, but for you to be encouraged by recalling God's goodness. I love to see increased miracles and see them more often. However, I also am reminded that the Pharisees demanded more signs and wonders even from Jesus! So, we might draw some understanding from this worldly perspective of judgment. Specifically, that if some people could not even be satisfied with the miracles and signs which Jesus did, why would you try to impress them or convince them of the validity of your ministry through signs and miracles? God doesn't, so why should we?

When Jesus left His commission with His apostles and disciples, He said in Mark 16:17-18, *"And these signs shall follow them that believe; In my name shall they cast out devils; they shall speak with new tongues; They shall take up serpents; and if they drink any deadly thing, it shall not hurt them; they shall lay hands on the sick, and they shall recover."* The only requirement the Lord gave for these signs was to believe. Those who would have faith to accomplish these things in His name (his authority), would be known as believers. I sometimes jokingly say that we should prefer people become believers before they become leaders. I hope you get my point.

Consider that these signs, wonders and miracles are not signs of apostleship, according to Jesus; these are just the "regular kind of every day signs." The signs Paul was speaking of were of the same general variety, but they were accomplished in the course of his apostolic ministry. There is one thing which I notice that is often overlooked in 2 Cor. 12:12. Paul began his list with patience, not with miracles. Now the word translated patience in this verse is translated perseverance in other translations. Nevertheless, I point it out to you because I believe it is an attribute which Paul was using to set apart his apostleship from the everyday, garden variety, generally-willing-to-be-martyred-at-a-moment's-notice, testify-for-Jesus, first century Christian attitude.

Once I was speaking with a young man who was going through what you might call a "rebellious stage." He had decided that he no longer believed in apostles and prophets because he wasn't seeing "enough miracles." His proof text was 2 Cor. 12:12. I pointed out Mark 16:17, 18, and reminded him that all saints should manifest supernatural signs and wonders, and that a difference in the two texts was that Paul pointed to his patience. I then reminded the young man, with a loving smile, that those around him were currently exercising great patience with him. He thought for a moment and then agreed and added that he knew he was only saved and alive because of the miracles of God.

In short, I am saying that Paul was pointing to apostolic character before signs (but not in place of them). If we look only for supernatural signs first and foremost, I believe we will place ourselves in danger of eventually being deceived, led astray, or, in the least, hurt unnecessarily.

Am I saying that signs are unimportant? Not at all, simply that I look for the character of Christ first. After all, in the heart of every true minister is the desire that Christ would be formed in His people. How on earth - or in heaven - can one assist Christ being formed in His people if His character is not first being formed in the minister? Could Paul say, *"Imitate me, just as I also imitate Christ"* (1 Cor. 11:1, NKJV) if he were not imitating Him closely? Jesus said simply concerning disciples and ministers that we could know them by their fruit.

FRUIT MUST REMAIN

When I was younger, I was more willing to overlook questionable character traits in ministers because I saw supernatural power and the fruit which appeared to accompany that power. Over time, and a lot of hard-won learning, I found that a lot of the fruit did not remain, and also some of what I thought was fruit was not nutritious at all. I sought the Lord on this question. I was seeking a way to discern much more quickly the fruit in a ministry so I would not have to expend so much time, and often experience so much hurt and disappointment. May I share with you what His Spirit said to me? He said simply, "You will know them by their fruit."

Now I had a dilemma. I thought I was right back where I had begun, and then it dawned on me that I'd been looking at the fruit from the ministry, rather than the fruit from the minister. There is an important difference. Paul said, *"But the fruit of the Spirit is love, joy, peace, patience, kindness, goodness, faithfulness, gentleness, self-control; against such things there is no law"* (Gal. 5:22, NASB). I now realize that I can look for these attributes in the minister's life and spend a lot less time deciding if I would submit myself to the ministry. Now I spend a lot less time in disappointment from a minister who "did me wrong," or led me wrong. I simply do not submit myself to a ministry where I do not see the character of Christ more clearly exemplified than any other attributes.

Am I saying that a minister cannot be from God if they are not exhibiting the fruit of the Spirit? No, not at all. Once I was crying out to the Lord about a particular minister who had become somewhat of a "thorn in the flesh" to me in a number of ways. I was surprised when the Lord answered me by saying that He used arrogant, controlling people to get work done all the time.

During one season, I had poured my heart and all I had into establishing a work of ministry in an Asian nation where the Lord had sent me. Later another minister, who called himself an apostle, came in and drew many after himself by teaching things which seemed good and helpful, but were contrary to the foundations which we had laid both apostolically and prophetically. In time, my heart was broken as I saw the church we had established follow after this man and his teachings, accepting the bribes which he offered subtly so that he could show "fruit" to his contributors back home.

I was troubled and I sought the Lord and He showed me a vision. In the vision I watched two carpenters who came to work on a building. One worked in pride and loud boisterousness, while one worked in humility of heart. At the end of the day, the Lord only paid the humble carpenter. Then I realized that the Lord as The Master Builder is going to put anyone to work on His building who can "swing a hammer." But, according to His own rule, if anyone does not work according to His plan, that person will have no inheritance (1 Cor. 3:14-15, 13:3; 2 Tim. 2:5; Gal. 5:21, etc.). In time I was asked back into relationship with the ministries that were affected by this man to help restore the people and the ministry, as a father would, from the hurt and damage that was done through the relationship with this person.

TRUE APOSTLES HAVE BEEN WITH JESUS

I am not saying that an apostle or any other minister must be perfect, only perfected. However, their character must be a foundation for the signs, and the signs are no replacement for character; this is especially true for apostles. I choose personally to disassociate myself from arrogant, self-promoting, controlling people, and other works of the flesh that I see. I love to associate with the humble, to be with those who promote Christ, and boast in the Lord, and glory in their own weaknesses.

When the apostles were brought before the rulers in Acts 4, it was because of a notable miracle. But the miracle did not convince the judges; what they took note of was "that these men had been with Jesus." I would like to think that the first impression received from an apostle would be "that person has been with Jesus." Paul said it best I think, and I borrow from his teachings (paraphrase) when I choose for myself: "While they might be an apostle unto others, they will not be unto me." When it comes to the signs of apostleship — character comes first. Matt. 23:11 states, *"But he that is greatest among you shall be your servant."*

ABOUT THE AUTHOR

Lloyd Phillips is director of Fellow Laborers' International Network (FLInt Net), and is committed to equipping the saints for Christian service. Traveling and teaching for more than 25 years in the United States and abroad, Lloyd seeks to establish God's divine order within the church, working with others to "both do and teach" in order to prepare the church as a glorious bride for the Lord Jesus Christ. Lloyd ministers the mystery and majesty of the glory of God through the message of intimacy with the Lord and preparing the Body of Christ for the many aspects of Kingdom authority and living.

Lloyd is a published author of *Growing in the Prophetic, Choose Your Weapon,* and many other articles in periodicals, books and publications. FLInt Net is an association of ministers and ministries joined together by desire and relationship, linked through the apostolic office, to fulfill divine purposes and callings of individuals and churches to complete the Great Commission. Lloyd believes that by being connected, each is better enabled to raise up, disciple, and equip God's people to do His work. His contact information is as follows:

Lloyd C. Phillips, Director; The Fellow Laborers' International Network (FLInt Net), P.O. Box 113, Missoula, MT 59806. Phone (406) 251-7035, email: flintnet@flintnet.org, Website: http://www.flintnet.org

CHAPTER THIRTY-SEVEN

SOCIETY OF LEADERS

MORRIS E. RUDDICK

"Arise, shine, for your light has come and the glory of the Lord has arisen upon you. For darkness shall cover the earth and deep darkness the peoples. But the Lord has arisen over you and His glory will be seen upon you. Gentiles shall come to your light and kings to the brightness of your rising."
(Isa. 60:1-3)

INTRODUCTION

These are extraordinary times. They are times when knowing-what-to-do takes something more. Mounting turbulence in global affairs shouts that it no longer is business as usual. America is divided. China is pursuing economic dominance. Russia seems intent on regaining its role as bully. Iran is plowing a nuclear pathway. Israel has been targeted for annihilation. International economies are being blind-sided with short-term fixes. Globally, beguiling policies mask realities. Terrorism is a global threat and lawlessness abounds. In all this, more than two thirds of the world's population lives under what the Psalmist calls oppression, affliction and sorrow.

The issue is one of power, as the time-clock hastens toward the power shift of all ages, described by Isaiah.

"The abundance of the sea will be turned to you. The wealth of the nations will come to you."
(Isa. 60:5)

In the midst of the churning, God has a plan and a strategy. It involves a dimension of "something more" than the best of what the world has to offer.

This something more has historical precedent with the biblical heroes of faith. Joseph the Patriarch demonstrated it under the most adverse of circumstances. Daniel exercised it when immersed in a culture of sorcery. David, as a most unlikely candidate, prevailed with it and ushered his people into a time of great unity and peace.

The mark of the "something more" is neither position nor throwing large amounts of funding at the problem. The something more is a factor of leadership—an influence that brings change from within. Despite Joseph and Daniel being slaves, they never gave in to a slave's heart. As wise stewards of their mantle they faithfully served, and brought God into the equation as they were blessed to be a blessing and in the process wielded change that released God's purposes.

The "something more" is at the heart of biblical leadership. It is foundational to the apostolic mantle.

A MOST UNLIKELY PEOPLE

The "something more" required to make a difference begins with discerning the strategy God gave the Jewish people, which has enabled them to not only retain their identity, but with disproportionate achievement, to serve as catalysts and influencers to the civilizations that would rise and fall around them, like the Greeks, the Romans, the Assyrians, the Ottomans, etc.

We live in a world seduced. It is a world in which the perception is deemed the reality; where black is seen as white and evil is considered good. The Bible refers to this as the "bondage of corruption." Yet, from the beginning God has had an answer through those known by His Name who, through Him, have been, are and will be a light to the world.

Over the ages, the Jewish people have fulfilled the words of Moses that they would be the head and not the tail. Today with only one-fourth of one percent of the world's population, 27% of all Nobel laureates have gone to Jews since 1950. As a people, Jews have been disproportionate achievers and contributors.

Historically, in civilizations without a middle class, the Jewish people have served that function, as merchants and bankers and people of business. They have been advisors to kings, rulers and leaders and financed national agendas in the societies in which they lived.

Yet, as a people, the Jewish people have been distinctive. As a people, they have released nuggets of wisdom from God's Word that have become the foundations economically, governmentally, judicially, and morally for what we now call Western civilization. Jewish strategies have resulted in them outliving, as a people, the civilizations of which they have been a part.

A MOST UNLIKELY STRATEGY

The something more involves a leadership strategy that defies the wisdom of the world; indeed, it accesses and applies the wisdom of the ages. It is the strategy that drives the apostolic movement. Driven by the spiritual, it joins together community to operate as one with the economic. It is a strategy that merges an identity, a spiritual maturity driven by trust and discipline, along with a unique power to form a leadership—all of which is demonstrated "as a people." It is a strategy of righteous power in a corrupt world.

Righteous power builds and brings increase; it wields influence, and is a catalyst for opportunity that brings blessing to those in its sphere.

This leadership strategy begins with a grasp of God's purpose for His own (Gen. 1), to exercise dominion and subdue the earth. Then, with an identity and faith in God, as demonstrated by Noah, Abraham, Jacob, Joseph, Moses, David and many other heroes of faith, the mantle is gleaned from Abraham, to be blessed to be a blessing. The model also is from Abraham: of the God-centered, entrepreneurial community.

Within the community of God's people will operate the progressive stewardship of the gifts of its members. Prov. 31 describes this community-focused entrepreneurial dynamic. The process was outlined by Moses, with a focus on order, ownership and increase.

Deut. 17 outlines the discipline required for leaders, which carries an emphasis of embracing and constantly living according to the principles of God's word. Then from Moses' father-in-law Jethro, are the steps within the community to nurture and develop leaders. These combined dynamics represent the foundation of Jewish roots and culture from which the strategy of biblical leadership is derived.

FOUNDATIONS OF JEWISH CULTURE

These foundations begin by depending on God and responding to Him with an excellence in employing the model and the mantle. It operates with an identity of being a culture within a culture. It is a nurtured community that expands and builds itself up through trust and tz-dakah.

Its nature is entrepreneurial with a combined thrust of work, service and faith. Its government is self-regulated and originally designed to be self-sustaining. Increase results from the stewardship and service derived from the confluence of the combined gifts of its members.

It exerts leadership on the surrounding community through God-centered wisdom, service and influence. Its advantage is the spiritual authority to employ righteous power within the world's structure, with an impact that like Daniel, holds the potential of being 10 times better than the best the world has.

In short, these foundations of an identity, maturity, power and leadership "as a people" are God-centered. The result actuates the impact outlined by Moses in Deut. 28:15 of being *"the head and not the tail."*

In addressing the realities and turmoil of the times, the growing disparity between light and darkness point to the need to pulling it together in applying righteous power in a corrupt world.

"In the time of the end, many shall be purified and refined,
but the wicked shall do wickedly and none of the wicked shall
understand; but the wise shall understand. Those who are
wise shall shine like the brightness of the sky, and those who
lead many to righteousness, like the stars forever and ever."
(Dan. 12:3, 10-12)

COMPLETING IT ALL

Jesus came to do just that: to bring fulfillment, completion
to the foundations found in the Jewish roots of the faith.

"I came not to destroy the law and the prophets, but to fulfill."
(Matt. 5:17)

Punctuating the long-accepted strategy of the Jewish
people being a culture within a culture, He noted the
importance of our distinctive identity within the world.

"You will be in the world, but not of the world."
(John 17:15, 16)

Jesus went on to warn us of the challenges of being a
unique people of God.

"These things have I spoken to you, that in Me you might
have peace. In the world you will have tribulation, but take
courage, I have overcome the world."
(John 16:33)

He also made it clear that the mantle of Abraham, to be
blessed to be a blessing, would require our light to shine
clearly in the world, in order to point the way to God.

"Let your light so shine before men, that they may see your

good works and glorify your Father in Heaven."
(Matt. 5:16)

As these factors work together, God's people are called to transform peoples and nations by teaching them the principles of righteous power by which we all are to live. These principles are what He referred to as the principles of the Kingdom.

"Go, make disciples of the nations, teaching them to observe
all I have shown you."
(Matt. 28:19, 20)

The pathway of the Kingdom is as a paradox to the way the world operates. Its focus on God's power rather than ours underlies the premise that in our weakness, His strength is manifested. It incorporates an identity of not being like everyone else.

It is a culture of honor that is derived from humility. Its people share a purpose of making their assets work for them (parable of the talents). It stresses ownership without greed, in which ownership increases by sharing. It demands service by which growth comes by generosity: by giving to others. Ambition and destiny are defined by losing your life to find it (dying to self) and advancement coming by yielding. Leadership is demonstrated by serving. Change is brought about by influence. Finally, but not least, perfect love eliminates fear.

LEADERSHIP PATHWAY

Jesus came to restore the foundations, as it was in the beginning, with the model operated by Abraham. He came to lay an axe to the root of the alliance between the misguided religious elite and the corrupt rulers of the worldly realm.

Jesus came to impart the foundations for true leadership and the strategy and authority that would destroy the works of the devil and the bondage of corruption, to release God's Kingdom rule.

I once asked the Lord why the places He sent us with our economic community development program were such difficult spiritual environments. His answer was immediate and very clear: because His power is best demonstrated by the opportunity and change created in impossible situations. So, it has been with the examples shared in previous Internet posts.

BIBLICAL MODELS OF LEADERSHIP STRATEGY

Throughout the history of God's people, we have models of the impact made through God's leadership strategy. Abraham demonstrated it to the world around him with the God-centered entrepreneurial community model. Isaac (Gen. 26) was a light to the surrounding societies, when by heeding God's voice, he sowed in famine and against all odds reaped abundantly when no others were achieving growth.

Joseph the Patriarch, with a clear, God-centered identity, demonstrated the mantle of being blessed to be a blessing (Gen. 39), and became a catalyst of influence in harnessing the resources necessary to give refuge to God's people and bless the Egyptians in the process. Moses outlined the community response for God's people, as a people, in giving strict heed to the voice of the Lord (Ex. 15).

David embraced God's heart as the pathway of his destiny and brought God's people into a time of Kingdom rule. Hezekiah brought restoration, liberty and spiritual authority to God's people against numerically more powerful foes. Daniel reshaped and redirected the spiritual climate of the society of which he was a part. Nehemiah gleaned the favor to gain access to the resources of the worldly realm needed for restoring God's people to their roots.

A SOCIETY OF LEADERS

In short, we are not called to be or to operate like everyone else. We are called to be in the world, but not of the world. We're called to be the head and not the tail and to make a difference and to bring change.

Apostolic Kingdom leaders replicate themselves and mobilize community. They are paradoxes to the way the world operates and employs power.

God's footprint over the ages has been ordinary people doing extraordinary things through the simple things that confound the wise. From this has come the "something more" dimension: a leadership exhibited by God's most unlikely candidates, employing God's most unlikely strategies, that has brought about the most unexpected results when those known by His Name achieve the maturity to operate as a society of leaders.

At the core of this strategy is righteous power: the power to overcome the impossible. Paul gave a glimpse of the outcome of this Jewish leadership strategy as releasing the power that would raise the dead (Rom. 11:15). Isaiah similarly described a people (Isa. 58:10, 12) who would operate with a power to rebuild the ancient walls and be the repairers of the breach – implying a mantle, and spirit, with the ability to fix virtually anything.

"Teach them the principles and precepts and show them the path in which they must walk; then give them the work they must do. Then select from all the people able men, such as fear God, men of truth, hating covetousness; and make them to be rulers of thousands, of hundreds, of fifties, and of tens" (Ex. 18:20-21).

Editor's Note: This chapter has been adapted from "Righteous Power in a Corrupt World" and used with permission of the author.)

ABOUT THE AUTHOR

Morris E. Ruddick has been a forerunner and spokesman for the call of God in the marketplace. He is the founder of the God's Economy Entrepreneurial program, which imparts hope and equips economic community builders where God's light is dim in both the Western and non-Western world. He is also author of four books: *The Joseph-Daniel Calling; God's Economy, Israel and the Nations; The Heart of a King*; and *Something More*, which address the mobilization of apostolic business and governmental leaders called to impact their communities with God's blessings. To learn more or contact Morris, visit his websites at www.strategic-initiatives.org or www.ruddickintl.com.

CHAPTER THIRTY-EIGHT

THE MARKS OF AN APOSTLE

KARI BROWNING

What are the marks of a true apostle? My hope and prayer is that you, the reader, will learn to discern true apostles from those falsely claiming to be apostles. The Church at Ephesus was commended for this:

> *"I know that you cannot tolerate wicked men, that you have tested those who claim to be apostles but are not, and have found them false."*
> (Rev. 2:2, NIV, author's emphasis)

To begin with, there are specific characteristics that clearly mark an apostle in Scripture, including two that I will focus on here: *Signs, Wonders and Miracles* and *Suffering*.

SIGNS, WONDERS AND MIRACLES

> *"The things that mark an apostle – signs, wonders and miracles – were done among you with great perseverance."*
> (2 Cor. 12:12, NIV, author's emphasis)

*"The apostles performed many miraculous signs and
wonders among the people."*
(Acts 5:12a, NIV, author's emphasis)

I have a friend, named Bob Jones, who is considered by
many to be a modern-day prophet. On July 3, 1984, he had
an encounter with the Lord where he saw the "apostolic
coming forth." Bob saw a group of 35 young people carrying
the Ark of the Covenant to Arrowhead Stadium in Kansas
City. They were leading a great procession of people who'd
been healed due to their ministry. The Lord said to Bob:
"These young ones are those who will keep me high and
lifted up all the days of their lives! I'll prepare them to bring
the glory of God in. They'll bring it in through Isaiah 35, the
Highway of Holiness. They'll serve the Lord all the days of
their lives and be faithful to the end." I am longing for that
day and I believe it is near!

*"The desert and the parched land will be glad...they will
see the glory of the LORD, the splendor of our God. Then
will the eyes of the blind be opened and the ears of the deaf
unstopped. Then will the lame leap like a deer, and the
mute tongue shout for joy...and a highway will be there;
it will be called the Highway of Holiness"* (Isa. 35:1,5 & 8,
NIV, author's emphasis)

On March 3, 2003, the ministry I oversaw hosted a
conference and prophetic roundtable in Coeur d'Alene,
Idaho, titled "Revelation Glory." After selecting the date
(because of a sign we'd been given about change coming
on March 3, 2003), Benny Hinn was on TBN and he began
to prophesy of a "mighty change" coming and it would
begin on March 3! For us it was an amazing confirmation
to the revelation we received. Several speakers taught at

our conference, including Bob Jones, Shawn Bolz, Bobby Conner, Ray Hughes, Noel Alexander, and Paul Keith Davis.

While attending our conference, Ray Hughes had a dream. In it, he was digging up potatoes in Idaho and placing them in a bag. Each one turned into little apples! Bob Jones appeared in the dream and said to Ray, "It's the apple-stolic!" Then the label on the bag changed from "Idaho" to "Ida-hope." Can God be amusing? I know so!

Have you ever had a calendar date become holy to you? *Read on!* It's interesting to note that Bob Jones had this encounter (about the apostolic coming forth) on July 3, 1984. God had told him years before that He would visit him on July 3rd with an important message, plus there'd be a *double* rainbow on that day to confirm the revelation and there was. Besides this, I found out that Idaho became a state on July 3, 1890. And, it was also on July 3, 1991 that God spoke to me *audibly* to move to Idaho. *Mere coincidences – I think not!*

I believe I've been given a mandate to trumpet the message of change coming by the restoration of the apostolic ministry. I believe the "apples" were small in the dream because the apostolic ministry was just beginning to be restored in 2003. But, we'll see it fully mature before the end of the age. This should give us great hope.

Exactly three years later, on March 3, 2006, we brought all the same speakers back for a conference entitled, "It's Time – Releasing Apostolic Power." In preparing the brochure for that conference, I instructed my secretary to use an illustration of neon green apples to symbolize the "apple-stolic." After giving that instruction, I went to a lunch appointment where a holy surprise awaited me! I was to meet a woman who'd just moved to the area from Ireland. She didn't know about Ray's dream, but get this – while shopping that day, God told her to buy me a neon green apple! The woman handed me the gift with a bewildered look on her face, saying, "God said you would know what it meant!" I sure did!

SOUTH AFRICAN VIOLET AND NATION TRANSFER OF SPIRITUAL GIFTS

"The government in the future will be decided on the indisputable fact of signs and wonders." Noel Alexander made that statement at the Revelation Glory conference in 2003 and I've never forgotten it.

Noel Alexander is originally from South Africa and now resides in Kansas City. Years before meeting Noel, Bob Jones prophesied, "When Major General Alexander comes it will be the beginning of the government of the movement." He was referring to the prophetic, prayer and youth movement that began in Kansas City.

I was invited to speak at a conference in Port Elizabeth, South Africa, in April 2000, entitled "Moving into the Apostolic." Before leaving for South Africa, I insisted that Noel pray for me – and I was sure glad he did! He prayed that signs and wonders would manifest from the moment I stepped onto the soil of his beloved homeland. What a prayer! And...his prayer was answered on that trip, and eight other subsequent trips I've made to South Africa.

Prior to my first trip to South Africa, Bob Jones had a word on the *Elijah List*, stating that he'd seen a vision of a South African Violet. He interpreted the vision to mean "the gifts of the Holy Spirit that were present in South Africa were going to be transferred to the American Church." Wow!

Before going to South Africa, I heard amazing reports of "feathers" appearing in meetings in the United States. Bob Jones said "the appearance of feathers were parabolic and God was using them to make a feather pillow – because God was looking for a resting place." What a unique and fun picture!

"This is what the LORD says: 'Heaven is my throne, and the earth is my footstool. Where is the house you will build for me? Where will my resting place be?'"
(Isa. 66:1, NIV, author's emphasis)

After preaching my first message in South Africa, at a conference entitled "Moving into the Apostolic," I felt impressed to read Isaiah 60 out loud concerning glory. I then asked a psalmist to sing it prophetically over the congregation. To our amazement and awe, lots of feathers began to fall! What a sacred, precious display from Heaven that was! I believe the message conveyed through that particular sign and wonder was that there is rest for each of us in the glory realm. I believe the restoration of the apostolic ministry will usher in such rest and glory.

In 2002, I returned to South Africa and witnessed more glory manifestations after I was instructed in a dream to teach on the heavenly realm. We experienced gemstones manifesting in the church building, gold dust appearing on people, plus angels appearing and feeding people hot bread from heaven, people smelling fragrances, drunkenness in the Holy Spirit, and many reports of people being healed.

Sincerely, I was ruined for anything *less*. I continued to contend for the glory realm that I had so powerfully witnessed in South Africa to come to the United States. We experienced an outpouring of the glory realm in Coeur d'Alene, Idaho, four years later in 2006.

SOUTH AFRICA IS LEADING IN THE RESTORATION OF APOSTOLIC MINISTRY

If you didn't know, South Africa is a nation that is leading in the restoration of the apostolic ministry with signs, wonders, and miracles. My last trip to South Africa was to Durban in October 2009. The glory realm manifested on the last night of the conference while Randy DeMain, who functions in an apostolic role, ministered. Here are some outstanding examples: a glory cloud entered the room, it rained inside the building, and two of the worship leaders received dental miracles of gold and silver crowns, and several were healed. What a meeting! I believe there was a message in the signs:

> *"'The silver is mine and the gold is mine,' declares the Lord Almighty. 'The glory of this present house will be greater than the glory of the former house,' says the Lord Almighty."*
> (Hag. 2:8-9, NIV, author's emphasis)

Many years ago, when I was a new Christian, I asked my pastor if there were "apostles today." Maybe you've asked similar questions. He wasn't sure, and said he'd get back to me with an answer. But then, I found a book in the church library entitled, *Andrew Murray, Apostle of Abiding Love."* Andrew Murray was an *apostle* who championed revival in South Africa in 1860. I was hooked and bought all of his books that I could get my hands on.

John G. Lake, who was also a true modern apostle, went to South Africa in 1908 and in his ministry saw many notable signs, wonders and miracles. He was the founder of the Apostolic Faith Mission of South Africa and birthed over 600 Apostolic Faith churches there. After ministering five years in South Africa, he came to the area where I live and started the Spokane Healing Rooms where there were 100,000 documented healings in five years' time.

In 2001, I had the privilege of speaking in one of the churches John G. Lake founded in Cape Town. I taught on "re-digging the healing well of John G. Lake." Six years later, at the *exact date and time* that I received that message for the Apostolic Faith church, the recently appointed Directors of the Healing Rooms in South Africa, arrived to transport me to speak at their Vineyard church in Cape Town. There were no Healing Rooms established in South Africa when I gave the message in 2001. I knew it wasn't a "coincidence" that the Healing Rooms, Directors picked me up on the exact date and time that I had received the message to re-dig the healing well of John G. Lake six years prior. I love how God confirms His word with signs.

"Then the disciples went out and preached everywhere, and the Lord worked with them and confirmed his word by the signs that accompanied it."
(Mark 16:20, NIV, author's emphasis)

MODERN EVENTS IN THE SPIRITUAL HISTORY OF SOUTH AFRICA

More little known facts about South Africa's modern spiritual history include the following:

Rees Howell, the great Welsh intercessor (who was a part of the Welsh revival of 1904), went to South Africa after having married in 1910. It was a costly emotional sacrifice because it meant leaving his newly-born son in Wales. He experienced revival in South Africa and saw many thousands make decisions for Christ.

Rodney Howard-Browne, who was the catalyst for what was known as "the laughing revival," that ultimately sparked the 1994 "Toronto Blessing," is from South Africa.

William Branham, the catalyst for the Latter Rain Revival of the 1940s and '50s, had his greatest meetings in South Africa. Meetings were conducted in 11 cities with a combined attendance of a half million people! On the final day of the Durban meetings, an estimated 45,000 people attended and thousands were turned away. Great miracles took place – the deaf heard, the lame walked, and the blind saw! I personally met an elderly woman in South Africa who was miraculously raised from her deathbed in one of William Branham's meetings while in her teenage years.

William Branham was instructed by an angel not to leave Durban and to continue the meetings there. He did not obey the voice of the angel because of pressure from those managing his campaign. They wanted him to move on to fulfill other commitments that had been made. Branham almost lost his life for his disobedience and he greatly regretted his decision. Because of Branham's disobedience, there was still unfinished business in Durban.

Get this! After preaching in Durban in 2008, I had a strong impression that Randy Clark (a former Vineyard pastor who was powerfully touched in a Rodney Howard-Browne meeting and was then used by God as the catalytic spark of the Toronto outpouring in 1994) was supposed to hold meetings in Durban. On my way home, I was divinely seated next to his intercessor on her flight home from a crusade in Brazil. She'd been interceding for his meetings there. I told her of the strong impression I had that Randy was to minister in Durban. She related that Randy was already feeling drawn to minister in South Africa. No coincidence here! In time, meetings were arranged for him in Durban the following year. Amazing healings took place and he has continued to return to Durban to minister.

On April 6, 2006, I was in a prayer meeting and someone saw a vision of the enemy holding a blue fireball. I instantly knew it represented the healing ministry of William Branham and we needed to recover it from the enemy's hands. I spoke forth the interpretation of the vision. After I left the prayer meeting, I listened to a teaching CD in my car. I had bought the CD the previous month in Topeka, Kan. at a conference where Jeff Jansen was ministering. I was astonished when Jeff began to relate a story about William Branham's birth and how a blue fireball had come into the room on the day he was born. Later, I discovered that April 6 was William Branham's actual birthdate.

Later that year, Jeff Jansen was given a prophetic word by a well-known prophet who actually had a face-to-face encounter with Jesus *concerning* Jeff. In this meeting, the prophet was given instructions to tell Jeff that if he would go to four cities in South Africa (Port Elizabeth, Durban, Cape Town, and Johannesburg) that the healing ministry of William Branham could be recovered. I had contacts in those four cities and told Jeff I could help set up meetings. I felt an affirmation on the prophetic promise because of the experience I had on April 6. I accompanied Jeff to the four cities to recover the healing mantle of William Branham.

We experienced many signs and wonders on that trip, including seeing the woman who had been healed from her deathbed in a Branham meeting many years prior, now receive a dental miracle of a gold crown! In the last city we visited, the intercessors symbolically hit the powerful blue fireball back to the United States.

In October, 2011, I was in a meeting with Dr. James Maloney in New Mexico. He was ministering very much like William Branham had decades ago. I wept as I realized that Dr. Maloney was the recipient of the prophetic promise that had been given in 2006 about the recovery of the blue fireball. An angel stands by Dr. Maloney when he ministers, as was the case with William Branham. He is regularly given panoramic visions and is able to tell people their physical conditions and other specific information that he has no way of knowing in the natural. He's witnessed numerous healings and notable creative miracles. Plus, he received a prophetic word 40 years ago that he would be given a gift that would be a catalytic spark for a new move of God. Dr. Maloney believes that this gift is for the "many" and not just the few and there will be other catalysts also. He is a shining example of a modern-day apostle that is moving in signs, wonders and miracles. I am thankful to know him as a friend.

The apostolic ministry, with signs and wonders and miracles, is being restored to a level of what was experienced in the early Church. There's an apostolic generation arising that will be marked by signs, wonders and miracles. It's time!

SUFFERING

"Finally, let no one cause me trouble, for I bear on my body the marks of Jesus."
(Gal. 6:17, NIV, author's emphasis)

> *"I want to know Christ and the power of his resurrection and the fellowship of sharing in his sufferings, becoming like him in his death...."*
> (Phil. 3:10, NIV, author's emphasis)

Does it seem to you, too, that everyone wants to be called an apostle these days? Another mark of a true apostle is suffering. I wonder if those who are calling themselves "apostles" are willing to pay the price of dying to their own ambition and agenda and are willing to enter into Christ's sufferings? Apostles must be prepared to lay their lives down in sacrificial love and to suffer, as it is part of the job description.

The apostle Paul said that he had worked much harder, had been jailed more often, had been beaten up more times than he could count and was at death's door, time after time. He was flogged five times with the Jews' 39 lashes, was beaten by Roman rods three times, and once was pummeled with rocks. He was shipwrecked three times, and was lost in the open sea for a night and a day. He experienced hard traveling, year-in and year-out, fording rivers, fending off robbers, and he had struggles with friends and struggles with foes. He was at risk in the city, at risk in the country, endangered by desert sun and sea storms, and don't forget – betrayed by those he thought were brothers and sisters. He knew drudgery and hard labor, had many a long and lonely night without sleep, missed many a meal, and was chilled by the cold. He also had the heartfelt daily pressures of all the churches he oversaw. (See 1 Cor. 11:23-29).

The original 12 apostles of the Messiah knew suffering, too. Philip, Bartholomew, Jude, and Simon were crucified. Peter made an outlandish choice – being crucified upside down! Why? Because he did not consider himself worthy to be crucified like Jesus. Andrew hung alive on a cross for two days, James was beheaded, Thomas was speared to death in India, Matthew killed with a sword, James was stoned and clubbed to death at age 90. Judas committed suicide. The only apostle who died a natural death was John. That was after he had survived being boiled in oil! He "whom Jesus loved" was exiled to the island of Patmos.

In addition to the original 12 apostles, Mark was dragged to death, Luke hung on an olive tree, and Matthias (who filled the place of Judas) was stoned to death. And the Apostle Paul? Beheaded by Nero in Rome!

KING DAVID AS A PICTURE AND TYPE OF APOSTOLIC MINISTRY

I see King David as a picture and type of apostolic ministry. True apostolic ministry will be known by their mature love and their willingness to lay their lives down for the next generation. King David supplied much of the materials for his son, Solomon, to build the temple and usher in the glory of God.

> *"A new government of love will be established in the venerable tradition of David."*
> (Isa. 16:5, MSG, author's emphasis)

King David was identified and anointed by the prophet Samuel. I believe that one of the functions of a prophet is to identify and anoint those in the apostolic ministry. Unfortunately, many prophets are calling "themselves" apostles, instead of identifying and recognizing the true apostles! Lord, help us!

It has been said: **"What the Jezebel spirit was to the prophetic ministry, the Absalom spirit will be to the apostolic ministry."** King David knew the bitter pain of betrayal when his son Absalom won the hearts of the people to himself and led a revolt against him. Sadly, I believe those called to the apostolic ministry will be required to swallow the bitter pill of betrayal. Graham Cooke, who operates in both an apostolic and prophetic function, once said that he has been stabbed in the back so many times that his middle name should be "colander."

In addition to David's son Absalom betraying him, his trusted counselor, Ahithophel, joined in the conspiracy. Ahithophel was Bathsheba's grandfather and it is believed that he may have been carrying an offense because of David's act of adultery with Bathsheba and the subsequent murder of her husband. Ahithophel counseled Absalom to have sex with his father's 10 concubines publicly to humiliate and dishonor David.

Not only did Ahithophel join in Absalom's revolt, but Saul's grandson Mephibosheth, to whom David had shown such kindness and mercy, was among those who joined Absalom. Sometimes it may feel like everyone has betrayed us, and that we are standing alone, but it is only teaching us to learn to seek God's approval over man's approval.

"If an enemy were insulting me, I could endure it; if a foe were rising against me, I could hide. But it is you, a man like myself, my companion, my close friend, with whom I once enjoyed sweet fellowship at the house of God..."
(Ps. 55:12-14, NIV, author's emphasis)

As David is fleeing Absalom, he encounters Shemei who curses him and hurls false accusations at David. Shemei starts hurling rocks and dirt at David and his party. In 2 Samuel 16:14, it says that they reach their destination totally exhausted. Josephus wrote, "David went on his way without troubling himself with Shimei." David trusted God to vindicate him. That is some faith!

If you are called to be an apostle, you will suffer betrayals and false accusations. It is all part of knowing Christ in the fellowship of His sufferings and it may be the tool that God will use to forge your character. As Graham Cooke says, "Have a nice death."

> *"For it seems to me that God has put us apostles on display at the end of the procession, like men condemned to die in the arena. We have been made a spectacle to the whole universe, to angels as well as to men. We are fools for Christ, but you are so wise in Christ! We are weak, but you are strong! You are honored, we are dishonored! To this very hour we go hungry and thirsty, we are in rags, we are brutally treated, we are homeless. We work hard with our own hands. When we are cursed, we bless; when we are persecuted, we endure it; when we are slandered, we answer kindly. Up to this moment we have become the scum of the earth, the refuse of the world."*
> (1 Cor. 4:9-13, NIV, author's emphasis)

God is restoring the gift of apostle to the Church in our time. The glorious apostolic generation, who will regularly experience signs, wonders and miracles, is arising. No disease known to man will stand before this end-time company that God has chosen. As we continue to see the restoration of the apostolic ministry with signs, wonders and miracles, we will also experience great suffering. Both are the marks of a true apostle.

ABOUT THE AUTHOR

Kari Browning was a senior pastor for 12 years, oversaw a regional training center for five years, and started a Bible college that trained and released over 300 students. She has been a speaker at many conferences both nationally and internationally. She is currently the visionary and director of New Renaissance Healing and Creativity Center, where the focus is on stirring creativity and teaching on both natural and supernatural healing. The Center hosts health retreats for those who need a place to come for rest and emotional or physical healing.

She is the co-director of Imagine Creativity Center, a Reggio-inspired preschool and daycare that is focused on the creative arts. She is on the board of directors of Created to Create, a discipleship ministry for young adults that is designed to encourage them to influence culture through fashion, film, graphic design, dance, music, writing, and other creative mediums. She has a passion to see the Church be the most creative place on the planet! She longs to see believers come into a place of mature love and wholeness in their spirit, soul, and body. She resides in Coeur d'Alene, Idaho, with her husband. Together they have four children and five grandchildren. To learn more or contact her, visit her website www.newrenaissance.us or email her at info@ newrenaissance.us.

CHAPTER THIRTY-NINE

ABIDING THROUGH THE PURGING AND PRUNING PROCESS

DR. DAVID ANDRADE

Everything we do in life, even a financial venture, will carry with it trials and testing.

1 Cor. 3:13 says, *"Every man's work shall be made manifest: for the day shall declare it, because it shall be revealed by fire; and the fire shall try every man's work of what sort it is."*

John 15:1-3 states, *"I am the true vine, and My Father is the vinedresser (husbandman).* "Every branch in Me that does not bear fruit He takes away [purges]; and every branch that bears fruit He prunes, that it may bear more fruit. "You are already clean because of the word which I have spoken to you..."*

The Holy Spirit employs trials to unveil areas that need our attention. These areas are open doors to the enemy that need closure, buttons the enemy uses to control our lives, wounds that say no to the love of Christ, hidden sin that needs His intervention of restoration and deliverance.

Trials are the Holy Spirit's spotlight focused on areas soon to be purged and pruned. Oh yes, this will be painful;

yet, one will never reach maturity until the Holy Spirit has worked His work in us.

Abiding is the engrafted life of the branch into the vine to receive the nourishment absorbed from the root. Each part of the vine performs a task; the root takes in nourishment, the vine supports the many branches with its life and each branch in turn produces the fruit.

If the branch cannot produce fruit it is dead. Its ability to transform nourishment into life and fruit is terminated and so it is PURGED away as unwanted dead weight. PRUNING, on the other hand, is the removal of weighty shoots that absorb nourishment of the vine and though they flaunt a lot of pretty leaves, will never produce any fruit. The eye of the skilled vinedresser knows the difference, so He takes those big shears and cuts away. This is painful to the branch that shows a slow recovery, then all at once springs forth into a stronger branch able to support larger and more plentiful fruit. So, the branch must go through everything the vine goes through; if you are a branch, hold on for your life: through the storms, winds, hail, rain, heat and cold, and of course, the purging and the pruning.

THE PURGING PROCESS

The Spirit of God quickens one to give up that which is contrary to Him, to all that disallows His presence. We think we are free because we exercise the liberty to say no. Yet, real freedom will not come until after His purging and His pruning. The husbandman purges all the dead weight from the vine that is diseased or saps needed nourishment and strength from the branches. Nothing must obstruct the development of new, fruit-bearing branches. Yes, what is about to be snipped may have been a vital, life-giving, fruitful branch in its heyday. We all like to tell our stories and pat ourselves on the back and hang our trophies on the wall for all to see. But, the husbandman is not finished with us yet! No, He is only taking a few minutes to sharpen His tool. As we talk our talk, we may be uncovering the Holy Spirit's next surgical removal. So, don't be surprised by what is about to go—Ouch!

SO TAKE HEART AND PRAISE HIM

He is skillfully shaping and fashioning you by the direction of the Father, into sons and daughters conformed into His image and likeness. What is it that so easily besets you? What obstructs your ability to be fashioned into the fullness of Christ? What do you hold on to, that says "no" to the Spirit of God? The Holy Spirit may allow one to be purged, stripped beyond one's ego until one cries "ruined" – humiliated until Jesus is ready to perform His creative wonder in us. Humiliation may be His fine surgical instrument. You see, Holy Spirit-administered humiliation is the Father's imprint that HE is really in control. So, if that's what it takes, "Ruin me, Lord!"

The Holy Spirit purges one to bear the fruit of righteousness (Mal. 3:3, 2 Tim. 2:19-21). The Holy Spirit is purging our hearts from all that obstructs His ability to work His powerful living Word into our being.

The Holy Spirit's fruit has a godly appearance. It looks, smells and tastes like Jesus. From the first mouth-watering bite, its fruit is unmistakable. Its savor beckons one to pay the extra price to taste it. The fruit bears the signature of its husbandman.

One need not guess which fruit one has set their eyes upon; its packaging is unmistakable; its appearance awesomely remarkable; its taste is simply a heavenly, out-of-this-world delight; it bears no appearance of death. And one bite of its nourishment bears forth its life-giving virtue. So, one who is fashioned by the master must submit to the hand of the Holy Spirit who plunges one's life from fruitless and lifeless to vibrant life. Those who will give Him their old life, He in exchange, and without reservation, infuses His new life into them. What a deal! One cannot live in that atmosphere long and not be changed! (2 Pet. 1:4-10).

THE HOLY SPIRIT AND TRIALS: EVERYTHING YOU DIDN'T WANT TO KNOW ABOUT THE PRUNING PROCESS

Did you ever have a dream as a youth? One day you leave home to pursue your life's labor. So, with youthful vitality and passion, you diligently prepare your course of life. Four years in Bible College and beyond and now you're ready, "Send me, Lord; I'm your man." You plunge your life into the work. You have finally found your joy, and the certainty of great benefit to the Kingdom of God. Then in a moment, "poof," it is torn from your grasp by some unforeseen event.

Your inward searching reveals that all of your motives were admirable. You have placed your best on the altar of God and for what? A spiritual death has taken place. Any thought to travel that road finds no place in mind, as your tattered soul says, "not for a long time to come." You have just met the precious trial of your faith. The vinedresser has just pruned you back all the way to the bare branch. All the leaf and incoming fruit lies on the ground to die. One peers upon it, lost, as the remains are carried away to be burned. What remains is the sense of abandonment and feelings that you have been "ripped off." It is hard to believe that the Master would allow this to one of His own faithful servants (1 Pet. 1:7).

SO TAKE HEART AND PRAISE HIM

The husbandman is at work sowing into you His divine purpose, further equipping you for the labor of your dream, calculating His design and fashioning for further harvests for generations to come, so feel privileged because He has chosen you worthy; that is what I said, "worthy." You have been planted into His special field, enlisted as it were into His boot camp. You may as well relax because His fashioning may take awhile. No, you have not done anything wrong. In fact, this trial has come because of what you have done right.

One is often drafted without warning. No, you are not out of the will of God. In fact, you are so dead center. It is best to say, "Here I am; cut away, Lord" and then sit back and praise Him in it and through it. What can be expected is that the aftermath will bring His greater anointing, authority, sensitivity to His voice and fruitfulness in ministry. Alleluia.... The Master knows that the fruit He desires of you is much greater than what you have ever thought possible.

The Master dresses each vine with His own personal creative touch, engrafting into the vine an intentional personality, henceforth taking on an instinctive conformed character. The vine's branches spring forth in a disciplined manner, so as to form the desired roughness, grow stouter, and yield branches capable of producing greater volume and mass for fruit bearing. Year by year, the growth is easier to manage. Branches that have borne tremendous fruit at the vines' early planting are not spared. Nothing is left but a few choice sturdy branches on the vine. Even those that remain take on the appearance that they have been visited by the butcher. But, the visible appearance does not reveal the internal metamorphosis. Nourishment must flow to the chosen branches on the vine. The vine, once glossy with leaf, with fruit hanging in abundance, may look tattered, even crucified and naked, as its remaining branches are tied to the stake. Consider if you will, the life of Jesus, using this analogy.

Heb. 5:7-9 says, *"Who in the days of His flesh, when He had offered up prayers and supplications with strong crying and tears unto Him that was able to save Him from death, was heard in that He feared. Though He was a Son, yet learned He obedience by the things which He suffered: And being made perfect, He became the author of eternal salvation unto all them that obey Him."*

SO TAKE HEART AND PRAISE HIM. The vine will soon take on a resurrection; the vine will soon bare larger and more bountiful fruit at each harvest generation.

At a chosen moment, the vine will enlarge twice its mass in size, then again and again. The vinedresser is not only projecting for the seasonal fruit production, but is at work calculating the steady fruition for many generations yet to come. The healthy growth of each vine is monitored and recorded year by year, so as to produce greater fruit than the year previous. The maturity of the entire vine must take place, so that one day this vine will provide planting that will fill the whole countryside with vine in its image and likeness. A sturdy vine must be fertilized, the hard soil softened, and a hollow created for irrigation to catch the much-needed rain.

THE WORK OF THE HOLY SPIRIT

The vine's roots must absorb both water and sunlight to expand its root base. Thin vines that have not increased in productivity are pulled out by the roots, replaced with plantings from the most productive vines, which will yield a pure, large, juicy, succulent grape. The fruit of each vine will be tasted to make sure that the constancy is compatible for the wine. The internal resurrection is profound as well, because the vine takes on a new nature. Instead of a disorderly growth of its virgin days, it bears the instinctive fashion, which has been born into it by its dresser (Heb. 6:7).

Bearing fruit comes by abiding in Christ (John 15:4-9). Branches that have been properly dressed will support 200 times their weight by volume in fruit. That is quite an abundance. Unlike a branch attached to the vine, a believer can walk away from the work of God at any time they choose. We can disallow the Spirit of God to work His work in us. This is why many believers will never go beyond infancy. Yes, the Holy Spirit will continue to change one's smelly diapers, bottle feed and give some attention when one whines, but such people will never reach maturity (Heb. 5:13-14) unless they change and grow up in Christ.

OTHER SCRIPTURE REFERENCES TO ABIDING IN CHRIST

He who believes [*piesto*] – trusts in, relies upon, grasps unto, adheres to, has confidence in, believes upon, – in Christ is abiding.

One in whom the Spirit of God lives is abiding. John 14:16 says, *"And I will pray the Father and He will send you another Comforter, that he may abide with you forever."* 1 John 2:6 states,

"He that says [he abides] in Him ought himself to walk, even as he walked."

One who loves unconditionally is abiding. 1 John 2:10 records, "He that loves his brother [abides in the light], and there is no occasion of stumbling in Him."

One in whom the word of God lives is abiding. 1 John 2:14 conveys, "I have written unto you, young men, because you are strong, and the word of God abides in you, and you have overcome the wicked one."

One who does the will of God is abiding. 1 John 2:17 communicates, "And the world passes away, and the lust thereof; but he that does the will of God [abides for ever.]"

When we do not waver from our confidence in God, we are abiding. 1 John 2:24 says, "Let that therefore abide in you, which you have heard from the beginning. If that which you have heard from the beginning shall remain in you, you also shall continue in the Son and in the Father."

When we give ear to the leading of the Holy Spirit's direction, we are abiding. 1 John 2:27 states, "But the anointing which you have received of Him abides in you, and you need not that any man teach you: but as the same anointing teaches you of all things."

When we learn to submit to the mentoring of the Spirit, we are abiding and this is truth, and is no lie, and even as it has taught you, [you shall abide in Him.] Abiding builds our confidence in God. 1 John 2:28 records, "And now little children [abide in him;] that when he shall appear, we may have confidence, and not be ashamed before him at His coming."

When we live a life of holiness we are abiding. 1 John 3:6 conveys, "*Whosoever [abides in Him] does not sin; whosoever sins has not seen Him, nor known Him.*"

One who loves his brother is abiding. 1 John 3:14 says, "*We know that we have passed from death unto life, because we love the brethren. He that loves not his brother [abides in death.]*"

One who lives a life of forgiveness is abiding. 1 John 3:15 emphasizes, "*Whosoever hates his brother is a murderer; and you know that no murderer has eternal life abiding in him.*"

One who keeps the Commandments of Jesus is abiding. 1 John 3:24 communicates, "*And he that keeps His commandments dwells in Him, and he in Him, and [hereby we know that He abides with us,] by the spirit which He has given us.*"

One who contends for the Doctrine of Christ is abiding. 2 John 9 notates, "*Whosoever transgresses, and abides not in the doctrine of Christ, has not God. He that abides in the doctrine of Christ, he has both the Father and the Son.*"

One who remains faithful to their call is abiding. 1 Cor. 7:24 states, "*Let every man, wherein he is called, therein abide with God.*"

What is difficult about this Holy Spirit process is that many resist, and bail out before the process is complete, so they return again and again to the same issues over and over. Each of us are free to say no, but letting the Holy Spirit perform His work in us, will release new freedom and close doors to the enemy, and from the pruning will come a great harvest of fruitfulness and righteousness.

ABOUT THE AUTHOR

David Andrade has successfully raised capital for private companies and authored and executed growth plans as the executive director of RTV International Ministries, a global missions organization of over 350 churches and other ministries which are focused on the harvest. His experience includes Radio Host on KFSG FM, the Foursquare International Radio station during the '80s, a staff writer with the *LA Voice*, Executive Director of *Real Life and Times*, and author of various books and procedure manuals.

David recently served as the Coordinating Overseer for the Line in the Sand prayer gathering at the Rose Bowl in Pasadena, Calif. on 11-11-11, and again Oct. 26-28, 2012 with three events at three locations on consecutive days at the Rose Bowl, Faith Dome, and Mott Auditorium. Dr. Andrade serves on the Board of Directors of Pray California and the California Listening Team, and coordinates the Global School of Prophets and Global Leadership Team, among other leadership roles. To learn more or contact Dr. Andrade, email him at prayunceasingly@juno.com.

APOSTOLIC EDUCATION

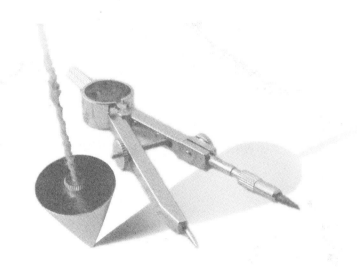

CHAPTER FORTY

THE CHURCH-BASED MANDATE: APOSTOLIC TRAINING MEGATRENDS IN THE GLOBAL CHURCH

DR. BERIN GILFILLAN

THE CHURCH-BASED MANDATE

My understanding of the role of apostolic ministry may be slightly different than others. The apostle Paul, during his day, put some boundaries on some of his apostolic influence when he said, *"If I am not an apostle to others, yet doubtless I am to you"* (1 Cor. 9:2). In the end, his message and mandates from God ended up being global and for the entire church age. To me, the apostolic anointing carries a heavenly authority and will bring new revelations, new instructions and new grace to those who will receive from it.

I know our ministry (Good Shepherd Ministries International) functions in the apostolic anointing, both in the marketplace and in the Church. The call of God we continually sound out is for every local church in the world to become a training center to prepare laborers for Christ's end-time harvest. The long-term goal we pursue is for local churches to equip workers and five-fold ministers for the purpose of church planting, evangelism and marketplace ministry.

Before I go further, I need to clarify my understanding of evangelism. Years ago I had the privilege of being the television producer for the evangelism ministry of Reinhard Bonnke. It was a great experience and although I have nothing against the wonderful Billy Graham-style crusades Reinhard conducts around the world, in which many millions have come to know the Lord, I no longer think that type of ministry best defines the church's task of evangelism. Instead, evangelism is defined to me by the mantra Dr. C. Peter Wagner drummed into my head during two years at Fuller Theological Seminary. He taught, with persuasive statistics, that "the most effective evangelism strategy under heaven is to plant new churches." This is why the objective of equipping laborers needs to be strategically focused on healthy church planting.

Years ago while visiting the Philippines, I received a prophetic word from the Lord that was very unusual. The Lord stated that He had placed upon my life "an electronic apostolic call to use the technology of our day to glorify His Name." This calling from God has manifested itself in our ministry's use of media and technology. We have used it to capture powerful teaching sessions from anointed five-fold leaders globally and to create a training equivalent of the "Jesus" movie for churches. Our International School of Ministry (ISOM) program currently is the world's largest video Bible school and is used in over 15,000 local church training sites. It currently can be found in 142 nations and there are more than 250,000 students receiving their training through it in over 70 different languages.

ISOM, for us, was only a start in the curriculum development task for God's training agenda for the Church.

ISOM was followed by the development of a translatable women's video curriculum (WOW), then a youth curriculum (YouthBytes), a community development curriculum (CDBoks) and finally a business training school (BTS). Undoubtedly, other curriculum will follow, but let's step back and look at the big picture. What is God apostolically speaking to the global Church and what is heaven's agenda and mandate? It's basically this: God wants **a mass training and equipping of an end-time harvest force and a perfecting of His saints through His Word to prepare for His coming.**

Let's look at the process. When God wanted to save and transform the world, we see in the Gospel of John chapter 1 that He sent **the Word**. The vast majority of the ministry of Christ was not healing, miracles or signs and wonders; it was **teaching**. The most neglected and least appreciated office of the five-fold ministry group is that of the TEACHER. Revelational teaching, not evangelism, prophecy or preaching, is what will bring about the purposes of heaven in these end times. Paul wrote in 1 Cor. 3:6, *"I planted (evangelism), Apollos watered, but God gave the increase."* Apollos was the one who watered and the Bible clearly defines him in Acts 18:25 as a **teacher**. That "watering" is what brought about the increase of heaven.

The development of the seed of salvation to a hundredfold multiplication requires the watering of revelational teaching. The planting Paul talked about is the "sinner's prayer" evangelism and it is a singular event, like a stadium crusade. That is where the Reinhard Bonnkes and the Billy Grahams come in. The Church loves that part because it happens in a moment of time and successes are easy to count, but the watering is where the real hard work comes in. It is a lengthy process over many years and it is only through that watering process that individual believers and the global Church are going to come to maturity. It is "the **washing** of water by the word" (Eph. 5:26, author's emphasis) that accomplishes the job.

If you want to transform the global Church, you have to bring revelatory teaching into the local church. That teaching has to be in a language the people can understand, it has to be revelational teaching from recognized five-fold teachers, and we have to use technology to deliver it in a way that does not violate biblical guidelines and biblical authority. The content of that teaching also is critical. It must carry a correct theology, a Spirit-filled message and a sound understanding of five-fold ministry, biblical structure and marketplace outreach. The local church is where new marketplace ministers should be incubated and prepared. It is not God's will to divorce the process from the local church; however, local churches need to take responsibility to embrace the task.

This is why our ministry continues to draw on mature teaching content from around the world and work to provide it to churches across the denominational spectrum globally. We have discovered that nobody has all the answers but by being Kingdom-minded and drawing on ministries of balance, integrity and fruitfulness, we are seeing marvelous fruit. I believe Dr. T. L. Osborn had a glimpse of how significant our undertaking was when he said years ago, *"As far as I know, the development of this (ISOM) Curriculum is the most important thing happening on the earth for the Kingdom of God today."*

The development of the content is only one part of the equation. The real apostolic task that has to accompany the content is how local churches utilize the content God is providing through our ministry and others to accomplish the purposes of heaven. This is where significant paradigm shifts need to happen and where God is bringing about major new training megatrends in the global Body of Christ. The remainder of my chapter will deal with these megatrends in training and teaching that I believe many will recognize and identify with. I must stress with each of these, that God is not removing the existing structures and systems; rather, he is adding to them these emerging megatrends.

SEVEN APOSTOLIC TRAINING MEGATRENDS THAT THE GLOBAL CHURCH NEEDS TO ALIGN WITH

1. To the traditional Bible training schools, seminaries and institutions, the Church needs to embrace the trend that God is adding a vast number of church-based and technologically-driven training entities. Let's start with church-based training. There is no better or more biblical way to multiply the training process than to add and recognize church-based schools and their graduates.

   This trend has to be embraced, not only by each local church, but also by movements and denominational structures. Instead of a denomination or movement with, for example, 500 churches having one main school in a country, they now can use technology to turn 300 of those churches into schools (with say 20 students in each). Instead of graduating only 200 students each year from their seminary, they can graduate an additional 6,000. What a massive increase in their leadership base for church planting, evangelism and marketplace ministry. The Internet and other media technology easily can make this possible. It either can be done through traditional media like DVDs or through live streaming webinars or through video on demand.

Our ministry is even using microchips smaller than a thumbnail to deliver training to remote and persecuted places. Each Micro SD chip can deliver close to 100 hours of training to the field. These chips also play in all Android phones and current statistics tell us over four billion people now have cell phone subscriptions. One must only look at the world statistics on Internet usage to understand this trend. In the year 2000, only 361 million people or 5.8% of the world had access to the Internet. By 2012, that number had risen to 2.4 billion or 34.3% of the world and climbing monthly. We are using this technology not only to deliver content globally but also for translation, reinforcement and review.

The main blockage or bottleneck with this trend is in denominations, churches and movements recognizing people trained through distance and Internet learning. Doing so may seem like an obvious step, but numerous groups still are refusing to give ministry credentials to those who are not trained through their traditional institutions. This often is due to internal political issues and power struggles as opposed to the quality of graduates. The apostle Paul in Acts 19 started a two-year, church-based training school and the Bible clearly states that from Ephesus *"all who dwelt in Asia heard the word of the Lord Jesus, both Jews and Greeks."* This reminds me of a famous quote I once heard concerning the early apostles. It went like this: "If they did what they did with what they had, imagine what we could do with what we have, if we had what they had." That's worth chewing on. Selah.

2. Taking our first trend even further, we need to understand that in addition to the urban training of believers, God is massively increasing the rural training potential of the Church and is instructing us to embrace the training of His people in the most unreached and remote regions of the world. The traditional model has been to bring believers from rural locations into the cities and even to sponsor them abroad.

   God is adding to that model, through technology, the ability to bring world-class training to the remotest villages in local languages. This enables those trained to immediately apply their knowledge into their local context and to spiritually and naturally transform their structures and systems. To align ourselves with this trend, our ministry has put together solar-powered projector and sound systems that are highly portable and can be carried into the remotest jungles to equip and train God's people. We have also initiated our Vision 2020 program to sponsor 20,000 training schools into the unreached and most impoverished regions of the world.

3. The third megatrend involves the kind of training being done to develop the next generation of leaders. Most traditional training institutions have focused largely on knowledge training. I believe God is challenging the Body of Christ to add to this model a stronger emphasis on mentorship and experiential training. Of the 28 qualifications for leadership in the Church outlined by the apostle Paul, 18 of them focus on character traits.

There is also a renewed focus happening in the area of gift development and anointing impartation. Traveling for over three years with Reinhard Bonnke taught me more about faith, leadership and spiritual impartation than 50 years at a seminary would have. Many online graduate schools, colleges and universities, and adult degree completion programs are now starting to grant credit for life experience. This is one way to align with this megatrend. Another is to actively include internships and practical experience in the training process. One school in Malaysia will not graduate a student until they have planted a church with at least 50 active members.

My daughter currently attends law school on the East Coast and has an outstanding professor who is actively mentoring her. This professor has created a special training program in Washington D.C. each summer that combines live teaching with internships and interactive mentorship. Such creative thinking is critical for the Church to adopt. Over the past decade our ministry has invested close to $2 million into the creation of a very dynamic, high quality curriculum for teenagers (www.YouthBytes.org). Probably no other project we have attempted has had more opposition and been more difficult to create.

We have filmed close to 50 episodes all over the world and used powerful national object lessons to drive home each message. In Thailand our host dressed up like a pirate and went into the markets to expose a message on what is real and what is fake. Nearly everything in those markets was pirated. We filmed the message on persecution in the Roman Coliseum and that of peer pressure in Sicily with our host joining the mafia. Egypt and its pyramids dealt with the afterlife and we flew to Japan to deal with teen suicide. Our *Sea of Trees* episode won a silver Telly award as we entered the 'suicide forest' at the base of Mt. Fuji and came across the body of a man who had hanged himself. From inside that forest where over 1,000 people have taken their lives, we spoke to young people one of the most powerful messages I have ever heard on the value of life. Such creative use of media and experientially relating to people is a key part of this megatrend that the Church needs to align with.

4. The fourth megatrend relates to gender. To the equipping of mostly male candidates for ministry and leadership, there is being added an intentional preparation of female candidates and ministry positions are being opened up alongside the men for them to go into. An Esther generation is starting to arise. Our ministry had a wake-up call when we read the statistic in David Aikman's book, *Jesus in Beijing,* that 80% of the Underground Church in China was female.

If the devil wanted to take out 80% of the harvest force, he would just have to convince Chinese Christians that women need to keep silent. This was one factor that prompted us to create a specific training curriculum for the equipping, empowerment and encouragement of women in the Body of Christ (WOW). It also prompted us to convene a huge conference in Europe with the theme "Men and Women, Side by Side." I preached on three partnerships, two of them from the book of Esther. She carried on her shoulders the salvation of a nation, not just any nation, but the Jewish nation, including the line of the Messiah. Her husband could have killed her for violating protocol but instead he held out the scepter to her and enabled her calling.

In a similar way David Meyer has enabled Joyce Meyer, Mark Zschech has enabled Darlene Zschech, and there are many other such examples. When Esther was granted authority, she immediately partnered with her spiritual father, Mordecai, and together they wrote the letters that saved her people. The third partnership clearly spoken about in Scripture is Aquila and Priscilla, who were a husband and wife team that ministered together.

Many such teams exist today such as John and Lisa Bevere, Brian and Bobbie Houston, John and Carol Arnott, Joel and Victoria Osteen, and numerous others. These three types of partnerships provide Biblical examples of an empowerment of women with which the Global Church needs to align itself. Others have recognized this such as Ed Silvoso, who wrote *Women: God's Secret Weapon*, and Bishop T.D. Jakes, who wrote the popular *Woman, Thou Art Loosed* book which has become a movie and conference seminar ministering to millions.

In addition, God still is raising up women all over the world to lead nations, major corporations, institutions, and even movements. One example was Aimee Simple McPherson, who started the entire Foursquare movement of churches. There is no question that women can carry strong apostolic anointings, and the global Church needs to align itself with what God is doing. Mary Kay Ash is an example of a modern day Lydia who founded, built and led a cosmetics empire that is still a global force today.

5. The fifth megatrend involves the revelation of the Church's role in the Seven Mountains of Society.

Although the vision of the Seven Mountains was given to YWAM's Loren Cunningham and Campus Crusade's Bill Bright back in the 1970s, it is people like Lance Wallnau and Johnny Enlow who have articulated in an apostolic way the application of that understanding to the Body of Christ today.

Those Seven Mountains are generally considered to be the education mountain, the political mountain, the business mountain, the arts and entertainment mountain, the media mountain, the church mountain and the family mountain. It is clearly understandable that whoever controls the high places of those mountains, controls the culture. It is also a truism that these mountains are very difficult to influence from without but much easier to influence from within.

Our ministry used to be primarily focused on training people within the church mountain. Over the past few years, we have aligned ourselves with the apostolic mandate to equip believers in all the mountains and to envision people to be promoted in whatever mountain they are currently in so they can influence their mountain for God's kingdom. It was after going through this teaching that my daughter, with tears in her eyes, said to me, "Dad, I wish everyone in my generation would watch this teaching: now I know it is God's will for me to go into law and politics. I can be used by God to influence those mountains for God's Kingdom." We as a ministry have put this teaching front and center in our training programs. We already are training lay people but now those who already are in mountains other than the church mountain have a whole new incentive to be trained in spiritual matters.

6. The sixth apostolic megatrend the global Church needs to align with pertains to funding. Traditionally, funding for the Gospel has taken place through charitable donations. There has been much teaching on how business people should fund ministry people for the purposes of heaven. I believe God is adding another dimension of new entrepreneurial strategies by ministry entities for the funding of the Gospel.

Recently, I was in the country of Swaziland where I came across the most unusual partnership. It was a joint venture between some high-powered business people in the country and an established ministry entity. Together they purchased an abandoned mining town of 4,000 acres. The entire town had been owned by a mining company and so they bought everything including 1,200 homes, the golf course, a conference center and all the surrounding land. They turned the town into a giant orphanage for victims of AIDS and started five businesses to sustain the work.

Although some of their funding is coming from donations, much is coming from their timber business, their bottled water business, their dairy, their bakery and the 1,000 beehives on the property. More than 300 children are being cared for but that is just the start. The project supports two schools, a life skills center, a church and over 1,500 jobs. There is a new synergy and integration happening and the Church needs to align itself with this kind of addition God is bringing to fund His projects. Our ministry in the past three years has purchased land and a beautiful building. Within the next year we plan to open a preschool, a juice bar and coffee shop, an exercise program, a full television facility and a high quality place to conduct weddings, banquets and events. We have drawn up a full business plan and expect it to be a strong part of funding our global missions endeavors in the years ahead.

7. Finally, there is a megatrend that deals with ageism in the church. Many times, in recent years, I have seen church movements so focused on looking youthful and on reaching young people that they actually push out those with years of wisdom. If you don't wear a certain kind of jeans and have a relevant haircut, you will not last long on the platform.

Other churches make no place for the youth and upcoming generation. When it comes to training, I believe God is adding both below the traditional spectrum of leadership training and is also going above it. The youngest student to matriculate through our ISOM Bible school started at the age of 9 and he graduated when he was 11. His mother would not let him register and get his own workbook until he had, using his mother's workbook, passed his first exam. In the end, he and his pastor were the only two students who never failed a test and his pastor admitted to nervously studying late so he would not be beaten by a kid.

I believe God wants a youthful Timothy generation trained powerfully in His Word and He also wants a Simeon and Anna generation mightily prepared for effectiveness in these end times. Within a month of graduating our youngest student in Lancaster, Calif., I was invited to a church in Pittsburg where I led the graduation for our oldest graduating student, who was a 91 year-old lady who had pastored a church for more than 50 years and was still pastoring with her son. I asked how she had enjoyed the training and she confirmed that she had spiritually grown wonderfully through our video training courses. So now, as I travel around the world, I challenge God's people that if they are between the ages of 9 and 91, they are being called into service for God's kingdom and need to be trained and equipped to be used in these end times.

In conclusion, there are many other such apostolic megatrends happening in the global church but I have tried to focus on some of the most important ones. These are all megatrends God is adding into the mix of what He is doing to prepare people for the Harvest and His coming. Our job is to recognize the apostolic mandate behind each of these and to align ourselves with these megatrends and with new technologies so we participate in God's purposes for our generation.

ABOUT THE AUTHOR

Dr. Berin Gilfillan founded and heads up Good Shepherd Ministries International, which is the producer of all the curriculum content described in this chapter. Dr. Berin did his undergraduate studies at the University of Michigan and his Masters at Regent University. He also did two years of study in missiology at Fuller Theological Seminary and holds a Doctorate from Vision International University. He is the author of the book *Unlocking the Abraham Promise* and his main website is www.isom.org. Find him also on Twitter @ceoisomorg and Facebook.com/ceoisomorg.

CHAPTER FORTY-ONE

EDUCATION & TRAINING FOR THE MARKETPLACE APOSTOLIC LEADERSHIP

DR. STAN E. DEKOVEN

In Dr. Peter Wagner's seminal work on the New Apostolic Reformation, *Church Quake* (pages 234-239), Dr. Wagner summarizes a most important trend in training men and women for ministry. A shift of monumental importance has occurred, moving theological education from the regional seminary to the local church, from the hallowed halls of academia to the streets where God's people live.

Dr. Wagner calls these new educational ministries "New Apostolic Schools," designed to create homegrown staff through innovative and radical teaching paradigms. These programs de-emphasize the gaining of degrees as the primary goal (options) at the expense of dynamic skill building. Further, Dr. Wagner lists seven key elements of these schools, which provide significant insight as to why they are effectively preparing leaders in the 21st century.

1. The training center in a New Apostolic School (NAS) is flexible in the faculty they choose. Rather than academic credentials alone to

determine competence, calling of God and empowerment by the Spirit are even more important. By and large, the local pastor will determine who teaches with guidance by educational experts they are in relationship with. Thus, a key tenet and principle of this approach is that...

2. Anointing counts as highly as degrees. However, most New Apostolic Schools will use men and women with a unique combination of both education and the ability to impart life. The instructors are challenged to teach head and heart in combination, using a very selective and flexible curriculum. This flexibility can be seen in...

3. A curriculum that is broad in perspective and centered on specific end results. The curriculum will generally include such standard courses as Old and New Testament, Hermeneutics, Homiletics and the like, but will also contain dynamic courses in practical ministry and such topics as Spiritual Warfare, Strategic Missions planning, and Deeper Life studies. Further, the New Apostolic Schools are...

4. Flexible in delivery system, which is designed more for the adult learner than the typical college student. The class schedule could be integrated within traditional Sunday school programs, Mid-Week services, or offered 1-2 nights a week as a part-time program, or even weekend seminars, combining dynamic instruction with distance learning. Further,

with the emergence of the Internet, many NAS are developing or networking with others to develop continuing education opportunities for people in their stream of ministry or network influence. Of course, the place for this instruction is...

5. The local church or the church in the locality. The Bible College or Training Institute comes under apostolic oversight, which provides the key governmental leadership to the school. In some locals, the NAS is actually a regional school sponsored and supported by key city leaders, a breeding ground for advanced unity in action, a most exciting phenomenon. Many of these schools are linked relationally...

6. In a voluntary relationship with other degree-granting schools. Finally, these schools are filled with...

7. The expectation that the graduates of their schools will be key leaders in the nations, filled with anticipation of great and wonderful things being done in the name of Jesus around the world.

The times are changing. The belief is that the world is reachable for Christ, more now than at any other time in history. We are asking the Lord of the Harvest for laborers, and New Apostolic Schools are putting feet to their prayers.

NETWORKS FOR TRAINING

There are wonderful changes taking place today in the Body of Christ. While many congregational and independent ministries are conducting business as usual, some are putting on new wineskins by establishing new ministry approaches, initiated by a season of unified, cooperative service in God's Kingdom for His greater purposes. This new paradigm, a return to New Testament Christianity, has been coined by Dr. C. Peter Wagner as the New Apostolic Reformation. A part of this new paradigm, or new wineskin, is the return of educational ministry to its proper and biblical roots: training in the local church.

Both in the world and in the church, the word "network" is being used to identify a revolutionary concept vital to fulfilling God's master plan. Networking, which is the willful and strategic working together in a win-win proposition, presents a glorious sign of divine life that will lead to the unprecedented revival we pray for and genuinely expect.

In 1990, God instructed us to start a network of Bible Colleges. Our mandate was to take "The Whole Word to the Whole World," bringing discipleship ministry to the nations. By faith we entered into covenant relationships with local church pastors possessing apostolic vision, whereby we (Vision) provide services to local congregations for the ministry training of God's people in a given community. This covenant relationship has proven to provide ongoing mutual blessing.

Recently, God has been challenging me to higher levels of leadership, along with greater revelation of His intentions in the 21st century.

I never intended to be a Bible College or Seminary instructor, let alone to start a non-traditional University with a worldwide network of church-based colleges. In fact, I was fairly content giving leadership to a large group counseling ministry, but God had other ideas!

In some ways, it was two "chance" encounters with two presidents of other Bible colleges which were in a network together that started me down this long eventful road. The most influential contact was with my dear friend Dr. Ken Chant. Dr Ken, an Australian by birth, was pastor of a problematic fellowship located across the freeway from my main counseling office. I had received a referral to counsel one of his flock, and called him out of professional courtesy and for good public relations. A few days later we met, thus beginning a wonderfully functional relationship.

Dr. Chant had crossed the waters of the Pacific to expand his teaching and writing ministry. He came to San Diego to establish his Vision Bible College program in what was then a large local church. The circumstances in that church deteriorated, but rising out of its ruins came Vision's present program, with the concept of taking this successful teaching ministry to the cities of the world. Under the direction of the Holy Spirit, we launched our network of schools, which now reaches over 140 nations, training thousands of leaders, bringing discipleship ministry to the nations for God's glory.

Our present and any future success will always be a result of calling and gifting, but primarily of God's grace. As the network has grown, so has our understanding of the theological and strategic importance of our work.

We are convinced, and would love to persuade every man and woman in leadership of the church, that every local church should have a Bible/Ministry Training Center.

Of course, this is my burning passion, created in my heart through the vision given me by the Lord, echoed in Hab. 2:14, *"For the earth will be filled with the knowledge of the glory of the LORD, as the waters cover the sea."*

It is my hope that you will take a serious look with me at the key reasons every local church should have a dynamic, Spirit-led Bible college program for the training of God's people, moving them into their individual gifting and calling.

The church in the locality is made up of all Bible-believing churches in a city or region…not just one congregation, though often there is a lead church to start the training program.

There are many wonderful institutions of higher education that train men and women for service: the best laboratory for training engineers, computer scientists, mathematicians, lawyers, etc., may well be a centralized university with ample resources. In like manner, the best laboratory for training Christian leaders for service within Jesus' Church is the local church in each city.

There are many excellent programs which will help establish such programs as ours, training leaders to fulfill the vision God has for them. We must follow the New Testament pattern of equipping people in local churches, and then releasing men and women of God into dynamic, life-changing ministry.

THE LACK OF LEADERS AND THE LOSS OF SONS AND DAUGHTERS

Over the past 15 years I have heard these two stories over and over again. The first is the lack of loyal leaders to work hand in hand with the pastor in the harvesting of souls. Pastors labor to win souls, preaching to them, counseling them in time of need, only to see them leave over some small offense, joining another congregation in the same city, starting the tragic cycle all over again.

Jesus told us to pray for laborers for His harvest, a prayer He intended to have answered through trained disciples (Matt. 9:10). The lack of leaders within the local church can be traced to the lack of a strategic plan to train leaders, due to faulty models, lack of resources or a wrong paradigm of ministry. All too often, in our transient society, people have been taught to cut and run whenever hard times come, demonstrating a lack of faithfulness and loyalty that fills the heart of leaders with dismay. It is a terrible and unnecessary loss!

Another tragedy I see occurs when the pastor, generally a man of high integrity, with a deep love for his flock, endures the loss of a spiritual son or daughter of the local church to a regional college or university. These gifted men of God have a vision to train leaders, and desire only the very best for their people, God's heritage.

Often the young man or woman has been saved in the local church and has been faithfully discipled by the local pastoral staff. However, when they reach age 18, and especially if a call of God is upon their life, a decision must be made as to where and how they are to be trained for full-time ministry or Christian service. Until recently, the only options were to send them to a regional training center, Bible College, or Liberal Arts University for their education. This has been justified as the "best we can do" for our young person, since our primary model for education has been the centralized, government-accredited programs that many pastors had to suffer with.

Since there have been few, if any, acceptable alternatives, the conscientious local church pastor would honestly attempt to assist the young person to make an informed decision as to which would be the best institution to attend. Unfortunately, horror stories are only too often the result. The stories include the stark reality that the once tender and hungry student in the local church becomes unteachable at best, and all too often they never return to the local church from which they came.

The causes of this phenomenon are many. They include the liberal agenda found in even the most conservative of regional colleges and universities. But this is only part of the problem. Add to this the agenda of the academic community at large, which has advocated the separation of the head from the heart, the Word from the Spirit. The focus of the regional school has only been the education of the mind, leaving little room for the training of the man and woman of God for the dynamics of a Spirit-filled ministry in a local assembly. Some notable quotes from a few expert resources might help to clarify just how problematic this situation truly is.

There have been four consequences to the scholastic, academic focus of seminaries:

1. The separation of Head from Heart.

2. The separation of Theological Education from Church Life and Ministry.

3. The Seminary has come to be viewed as a poor investment for ministry preparation.

4. Entrenched traditionalism has led to seminaries being structurally irreformable.

This started in North America at Harvard College in 1636. "Harvard College was created by the civil government and governed by a board of overseers, or trustees, made up equally of clergy and magistrates…[This followed the] Reformation model, which was one step more secular in the sense of being less directly under church control. The Reformers … depended on the princes for their success. Seminary founders … assumed that the day-by-day skills needed by the clergy would be learned in the give and take of [local church] community life. Nineteenth-century seminaries were the houses that theology built." (As quoted in *The History of Seminary Education and Theological Accreditation*, by Dr. Gary Greig, presented at the Apostolic Council for Educational Accountability, Colorado Springs, CO, June, 1999).

The standard models of seminary training are painfully out of touch with the average Christian. George Barna, President of The Barna Institute, reported (as presented in the provisional catalog of the Wagner Leadership Institute, 1998) as follows:

> "[M]ost pastors agree that they were inadequately trained for the job of leading the local church. Yet, seminaries continue to forge ahead, providing much of the same irrelevant (and in some cases, misleading and harmful) education that has been their forte for the past century. One response has been churches creating their own ministry education centers to raise up leaders and teachers from within their congregations. Another response has been for churches to hire believers who have secular training and experience in professional fields and allow them to learn the content of ministry realities while they are on the job. There is little doubt that churches are in desperate need of effective leadership as the challenges confronting the church become more complex, more numerous and more daunting.

"But how will those leaders be identified, developed and nurtured for effective ministry leadership? Is there a role for the seminary in the future of the church? If so, what should that seminary look like and what would its ideal role be? If churches continue to rely on seminaries—or some alternative developmental structure—to provide them with leaders, it is imperative that the leader training grounds be reshaped. Mere tinkering with a broken system won't provide the answer; creating a holistic, strategic, and intelligently-crafted process is needed."

This indictment against the "White Elephant" of standard seminary education has resulted in many new and exciting adaptations.

The very model of education and training recommended by our culture is different from and hostile to the model found in the Word of God. The New Testament model for education, especially preparation for ministry, is the apostolic pattern of training church leaders described in the Book of Acts. The pattern, detailed in chapter 4, is found in Acts, chapters 2 (Jerusalem), 11- and 13 (Antioch), 14 (Lystra, Iconium, and Pisidian Antioch) and 19 (Ephesus). Each city where Peter or Paul ministered became a discipleship or training center. When the proper vision of the great commission was in the forefront of the apostles' teaching, the church grew and God was glorified. This model is the only one that will reduce or eliminate the twin crises of a lack of leadership, and the tragedy of losing sons and daughters to the world or the regional, state-approved, often-too-liberal College or University.

The purpose of teaching is to be like the master.

THE WORD AND TEACHING

Teaching is the primary vehicle for the transmitting of cultural truth and biblical revelation from generation to generation. Throughout God's dealings with His people, He has commanded them to know the commandments and to teach them, so that all might live the commandments out in their daily experience. This process is supposed to continue from generation to generation.

In Ps. 143:10 the Word of God says, *"Teach me to do your will."* One of the primary purposes of the teaching ministry is to help people to know what the will of God is and then to do it. This teaching, as stated in Deut. 4:9, begins at the earliest age. It says, *"Teach them to your children."* Teaching and training is a process that begins in the family long before a child experiences a Sunday School Program, Children's Church, or attends a private Christian school. It is the responsibility of the parents to teach their children and to teach them well, with a primary purpose: To Win the Hearts.

Evangelism is to be a primary focus of teaching. Ps. 51:13 states, *"I will teach transgressors your ways."*

Everyone involved in local church leadership should have the ability to teach. That does not mean that each one is a gifted teacher, but they must be capable of communicating the truth of God's Word with clarity and purpose. Titus 2:1 states, *"You must teach what is in accord with sound doctrine (or sound teaching)."* Paul admonishes his son in the Lord, Titus, to teach properly and systematically so that a clear understanding of God's purposes for His people is gained. The teaching process is not to be mere "rambling-on" about whatever someone feels. It is a specific process of imparting divine truth found within the Word of Clod, bringing structural and permanent change in the lives of students. Thus, our focus is always to Equip the Saints.

A primary scripture that emphasizes the importance of teaching in the Christian church is Eph. 4:11. Here, Paul the Apostle teaches that the five-fold ministry, apostles, prophets, evangelists, pastors, and teachers are all necessary components in the ministry of perfecting the saints or bringing them to Christian maturity. The entire five-fold ministry, as elders, must be able to teach, imparting relevant truth from God's precious Word.

Also, in 1 Cor. 12:28 teaching is presented as one of the ministry gifts to the church. Thus, within the New Testament church, teaching was, and continues to be, a vital function to be exercised consistently. However, teaching is not teaching unless the student has demonstrated that they Have Learned.

The purpose of teaching should be to ensure that learning actually occurs. Just because someone is talking at the front of a classroom does not mean that learning is actually taking place. Probably the greatest thrill a teacher can have is to see the light come on in a learner's mind. No real teaching has taken place unless truth has become relevant to the student, which makes it applicable in their life. That is why learning is incomplete until it has become a part of the student's repertoire of knowledge and experience.

2 Tim. 3:7, KJV says, *"Ever learning, and never able to come to the knowledge of the truth."* That is the tragedy that many people experience. They spend much time in reading, studying and learning (not experiential), but never practicing what has been learned in a life of effective service.

Church leaders are to be sufficiently prepared so as to become effective transmitters of God's truth. This truth is to be applied by the student for active use in real life. In this regard, the Word of God speaks clearly and profoundly. A teacher is to:

"Study to show thyself approved unto God, a workman that needeth not to be ashamed, rightly dividing the word of truth" (2 Tim. 2:15, KJV).

"...because you know that we who teach will be judged more strictly" (Jas. 3:1).

"They want to be teachers of the law, but they do not know what they are talking about or what they so confidently affirm" (1 Tim. 1:7).

The teacher, functioning within a local church setting, with apostolic/pastoral authority, has an awesome and delightful responsibility! To equip God's people for His service in the kingdom is an honor indeed, and our labor is for His Reward.

It would be a great tragedy if, after a life of teaching, we stood before the Lord to hear Him state that what we had taught His people was only wood, hay, and stubble rather than gold, silver, and precious stones.

Heb. 5:12 says, *"In fact, though by this time you ought to be teachers, you need someone to teach you the elementary truths of God's word all over again. You need milk, not solid food!"*

There are many ways to view this Bible passage. Some commentators have stated that the "students" spoken of must have been dull or ignorant. However, perhaps the teaching methodology itself was ineffective, making the learning process for the student nearly impossible. I have seen that happen at times. If it was the apostle Paul who was doing the teaching, the assumption of dull and ignorant could possibly be assumed. However, not all teachers conduct their lessons with clarity and under the unction of the Holy Spirit. The conscientious teacher will seek to effectively and convincingly teach their charge, with the goal of pleasing the Master. This begins with being Student Centered.

When teaching, if the student is not learning, we dare not solely blame the student. It must be determined what possible weakness within the teacher or materials are limiting the effective communication of truth so a student cannot clearly understand it. The teacher is responsible for the communication, which should flow from the integrity of character in an instructor who is fully prepared, one who is Always Learning.

An educator must be fascinated with the learning process, for we never do obtain it all. The pursuit of knowledge should not be in vain, but focused on being constantly fresh, increasing our ability to impart new truth and revelation to open-hearted students. Therefore, we teach out of a heart of love and compassion for the students. This is to be done with recognition that every student will learn at a slightly different rate. That is why the teacher must be patient, fully aware of the differing needs of individuals, and able to effectively teach each one in submission to the Holy Spirit and the Word of God.

THE COMMISSION

When Jesus began His earthly ministry, He began as a *"teacher who has come from God,"* (John 3:1-2). This is not to minimize his role as Savior. He accomplished our salvation through His death on the cross and resurrection from the dead. But, His primary focus of ministry was to raise up leadership for the next generation. Thus, Jesus poured His life into His disciples, demonstrating for us a vital ministry principle, valid for today. In order to fulfill our purpose in ministry, we must learn to be effective in our teaching, having a similar focus in our teaching as did Christ. That purpose is to make disciples, preparing leadership for the outpouring of the Holy Spirit expected in every generation.

The first and primary reason for establishing the training of God's people in the local church is the commission given by Christ to His apostles. In Matt. 28:19, Jesus states: *"Therefore go and make disciples of all nations."*

Matthew 28 speaks about the authority that was given to Jesus in heaven and earth, and was subsequently given to His disciples. Their commission was to go forth and make disciples of the nations. The process they were to follow included the preaching the Word of God, baptizing in the name of the Father, The Son and the Holy Spirit, then teaching the converted to do all that Jesus commanded, all by the grace of God. God is with the teacher in the classroom as he or she submits to the Lordship of Christ. If we are in a place of authority to teach students, then we need not struggle to gain authority; we must simply act based upon our God-given mandate.

This "Ministry Mandate" was given to the apostles, to teach the principles of Christ until men and women could live as Christ intended. This mandate encompassed much more than just making new converts; it called for the discipleship of nations. That is, the nations were to be given the opportunity to receive or deny Christ and His supremacy. If received, they would also be grafted into the family of God, the covenant of Abraham. If not, the judgment of the Lord would be measured out to them, though His grace and mercy would give ample opportunity for repentance.

The disciples received that commission, though unfortunately they were limited in their vision to Jerusalem. Salvation for the Jews was their heart, though the Father's heart cry included the Gentiles. Throughout history, this commission has been transferred from one generation to the next, and we are the recipients of that same wonderful mandate. Thus, today we must recognize the commission's call on our lives, to continue the proclamation of the Gospel of Christ until the whole world is filled with the knowledge of the glory of the Lord *"as the waters cover the sea"* (Hab. 2:14).

As we can learn from the Book of Acts (Acts 1:8, 2:1-5; 47), the only way we can see the Kingdom of God expand is through the planting of indigenous New Testament churches. The work of the apostle and prophet, working together, provides the foundation and vision for the local community. This dynamic method of expanding the kingdom can only occur as young men and women are properly trained and equipped to go to the nations, full of faith and the Holy Spirit, able to speak with boldness the unsearchable riches of Christ. The commission of Christ mandates to us all to properly train men and women for Christian service, for local church and the workplace, and the New Testament laboratory for such training is the local church.

THE CHURCH: THE PLACE OF TRAINING

In our modern era, the local community church building is often the most underutilized space in the community. It is perfectly designed architecturally for multiple activities, including the teaching of theological subjects. Of course, the luxury of the type of facilities we enjoy today did not exist in Jesus' day. However, similar structures to local churches were used in the New Testament era for the training of believers.

In the New Testament, the most comprehensive picture of God's plan for training was modeled through the life of Christ. In John 3, Nicodemus made a very profound statement when he said: *"Rabbi, we know you are a teacher who has come from God. For no one could perform the miraculous signs you are doing if God were not with him."*

The primary focus of Christ's ministry was that of discipleship, or the transference of the Father's plan and purpose from His life into His disciples' lives. When they were finished with their educational program, the three and a half years they spent with Jesus here on earth, God's vision was for them to take up the mantle and carry on the traditions established by Christ. With this mantle they would be able to fully communicate everything that they had been taught and do everything that Jesus had done in the same way and the same measure that Jesus Himself did.

That should be the philosophical focus of every Christian leader. The education transmitted to a child or adult should produce life experiences with practical applications. When a child or adult has completed a class or program of training, they should be able to both communicate what they have learned and practice it in their daily lives. Thus, they become able to effectively develop their own potential to train others in the Lord.

Not only was teaching the focus of Jesus' ministry, but it became that of Paul the Apostle as well. In the Book of

Acts, Paul joins Barnabas the Apostle, sitting at Barnabas' feet as an assistant instructor (Acts 11). His tutelage under Barnabas continued for a full year, where they jointly taught the disciples in the principles of Christ. It was in Antioch that believers in Jesus Christ were first called Christians (little Christs). They must have had a fairly effective teaching program for such a visible change of identity and character to occur. A good assumption is that Paul and Barnabas taught everything that Barnabas had learned while he sat at the feet of the apostles in Jerusalem, prior to his being sent to spy out Antioch (Acts 11).

Later the apostle Paul continued in the same tradition. In the city of Ephesus (Acts 19), he focused his ministry on the disciples who followed him, and for two years he taught them. They rented a facility called the School of Tyrannus and there he daily instructed the disciples.

What did he teach? Everything Barnabas and he had taught in Antioch, which was a continuation of everything that the apostles taught in Jerusalem. This in turn, was essentially everything that Jesus had taught and modeled to them. This dynamic process, of one generation teaching the next generation the plans and purposes of God must continue in our churches today if we are going to see Christ's purposes fulfilled in the 21st Century.

THE NEW COVENANT GOAL

In 1 Tim. 1:5 we read, *"The goal of this command is love, which comes from a pure heart and a good conscience and a sincere faith."*

Paul's goal in teaching Timothy was to transform his life, changing his priorities. Timothy was one of the primary disciples of Paul, nurtured through Paul's teaching ministry.

In this verse, the goal of his instruction is presented. Paul's goal became the goal of Timothy's teaching ministry at Ephesus as well. The first and most important goal was love, which flowed from a pure heart. Secondly, a good conscience or developing the mind of Christ was essential, and third, a sincere faith, or a faith that was to be openly proclaimed by committed saints was to be the result of spiritual instruction.

PURE HEART

Paul's focus of instruction was not just to stimulate the intellect or to provide facts and figures, but to ensure a process of purification in the disciples' heart. The love of God was to be seen and expressed in the life of the believer. True love is to flow from a purified heart, one that has been changed by an encounter with the Spirit of God through the Word of God.

GOOD CONSCIENCE

"A good conscience" indicates that through the process of teaching and the study of God's Word, a change should begin to occur in the thought life of the student/believer. This change occurs as they look into the mirror of truth found in God's Word. As they compare their life to the Word of God, areas of deficiency in need of correction are revealed. As confession of sin or failure is accomplished and repentance is completed, the process of change takes effect. Ultimately, this process creates a clean and clear conscience, free from all guilt and anxiety related to these past mistakes or sins. Further, it changes our perception of life from self to being God focused.

SINCERE FAITH

Finally, a sincere faith is essential. This means faithfulness to the task that God has called us to. Whatever training a student is involved in, the expectation is that when they have completed it, they will be faithful to perform what they have been trained to do. It is not enough to learn something without making a practical application. Jesus taught with an eternal focus in mind. What the disciples saw Christ do, they did. Paul worked from the same central concept. It is vitally important for teachers as leaders to emphasize theory, theology and effective practice, faithful to perform according to the knowledge and skills acquired over time.

THE BIBLICAL PERSPECTIVE

As emphasized earlier, all instruction should be accomplished either within the home or through the auspices of the local church. This does not mean that other institutions are not serving the Lord and the primary focus of control of the educational process. The teacher must be able to teach to the best of their ability as commissioned by the Lord, according to the grace that God has given them and the measure of faith provided. Whether one is an active five-fold ministry member or has the gift, ability, and desire to teach, all need to do so to the best of their ability as commissioned by the Master Teacher Himself.

TO GROW UP

Referring back to Eph. 4:11-12, the concern or goal of instruction is to bring students to maturity. The focus of the teaching ministry of the apostle was precisely that. It was certainly the focus of Christ. If the focus was perfection, then both Jesus and Paul failed miserably. None of their students were paragons of perfection.

Their goal and ours is not perfection, but maturity. Maturity can be seen in the ability to rightly divide or understand God's truth and transmit it in spite of human frailties. Having the same concerns that God has for the students will assist us to remain on track despite our failures. The goals of instruction go far beyond teaching the brightest to shine (which they no doubt will do with us or without us), or attaining the highest grade point averages, but to ensure that the character of Christ is formed in the hearts of His people.

AN APOSTOLIC TEAM

The New Testament goal of teaching was to establish maturity in men and women and to create Apostolic Companies for future ministry expansion and church planting. When Paul or Peter ministered in a new city, their goal was to establish a teaching center and then a church (Acts 11, 13, 19). However, they did not go alone. They always took with them a team of trained leaders from a given city to assist in various aspects of ministry. Thus, when a church was planted, it was done by a team under apostolic and prophetic authority, built on a strong and sure foundation. They did not work with novices, but took adults fully trained in the local church for the expansion of the Kingdom of God.

In the 21st century, we must regain the perspective of the New Testament, and return to the philosophy of training found in the pages of God's Word. This can only be done through education and training in the local church.

PREPARATION FOR ACTIVATION

Of course, the reason for equipping/educating God's people is to activate them. By activation, I mean to see every believer emerge, through the teaching/impartation of God's word, with gifts to be used (see 1 Cor. 12:14-18, Eph. 4:11-16, Rom. 6-13) according to the measure of faith (Rom. 12:3) God has given.

Not all believers are called to church leadership, but all can serve, whether in the local church or the church in the workplace. It should be the goal of every spiritual leader to see the 80% of inactive Christians (according to Barna's latest statistics) activated into service.

A greater goal is to see the Kingdom of God expanded through church planting. Establishing New Testament churches everywhere is the key to revival. It is my hope that every local church congregation, cooperating with other congregations in the locality, work to see every believer trained, activated, and released into God's harvest field.

ABOUT THE AUTHOR

Stan E. DeKoven, Ph.D., M.F.T. is a licensed Marriage, Family and Child Therapist in San Diego, Calif., and a certified School Psychologist. Dr. DeKoven received his Bachelors degree in Psychology from San Diego State University, his Masters in Counseling from Webster University, and his Ph.D. in Counseling Psychology from the Professional School of Psychological Studies. He has also completed a Bachelors and Masters in Theology, and his Doctorate in Ministry from Evangelical Theological

Seminary. He is Founder and President of Vision International University in Ramona, Calif. and the International Training and Education Network. Dr. DeKoven is also the publisher and author of over 35 books in practical theology, counseling and leadership, and a popular conference speaker. To learn more or to contact him, visit his websites at www.drstandekoven.com or www. vision.edu or www. booksbyvision.com.

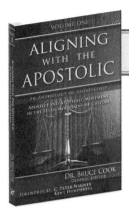

VOLUME ONE

ALIGNING WITH THE APOSTOLIC
A FIVE VOLUME ANTHOLOGY OF
APOSTLES & THE APOSTOLIC MOVEMENT
DR. BRUCE COOK, GENERAL EDITOR

Foreword by C. Peter Wagner
Foreword by Kent Humphreys

Volume One contains the Introduction and Overview to this historic work by 70 authors, written by General Editor, Dr. Bruce Cook. This volume contains an explanation of the research methodology used in compilation of the anthology and an extensive glossary of 80 apostolic terms.

VOLUME ONE

SECTION 1:
Introduction & Overview—
- Coming Into Apostolic Alignment
- What an Apostle Is, and Is Not
- Levels of Maturity and Types of Apostles
- Apostolic Authority: A Two-Edged Sword
- Origins of the Patriarchs & Judaism
  Are Found in the Marketplace
- Origins of the Church and Christianity
  Are Found in the Marketplace
- Apostolic Reformers in the Marketplace

www.KingdomHouse.net

KINGDOM HOUSE
PUBLISHING

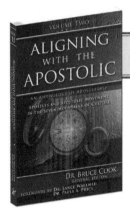

VOLUME TWO

ALIGNING WITH THE APOSTOLIC
A FIVE VOLUME ANTHOLOGY OF
APOSTLES & THE APOSTOLIC MOVEMENT
DR. BRUCE COOK, GENERAL EDITOR

Foreword by Dr. Lance Wallnau
Foreword by Dr. Paula A. Price

VOLUME TWO

SECTION 2:
Apostolic Government

SECTION 3:
Apostolic Foundations

www.KingdomHouse.net

KINGDOM HOUSE
PUBLISHING

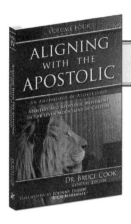

VOLUME FOUR

ALIGNING WITH THE APOSTOLIC
A FIVE VOLUME ANTHOLOGY OF
APOSTLES & THE APOSTOLIC MOVEMENT
DR. BRUCE COOK, GENERAL EDITOR

Foreword by Johnny Enlow
Foreword by Rich Marshall

VOLUME FOUR

SECTION 7:
Apostolic Fathers & Mothers

SECTION 8:
Apostolic Leadership & Teams

SECTION 9:
Apostolic Creativity
& Innovation

www.KingdomHouse.net

KINGDOM HOUSE
P U B L I S H I N G

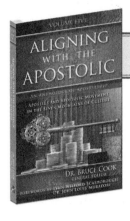

VOLUME FIVE

ALIGNING WITH THE APOSTOLIC
A FIVE VOLUME ANTHOLOGY OF
APOSTLES & THE APOSTOLIC MOVEMENT
DR. BRUCE COOK, GENERAL EDITOR

Foreword by Lynn Wilford Scarborough
Foreword by Dr. John Louis Muratori

VOLUME FIVE

SECTION 10:
Apostolic Multiplication & Wealth

SECTION 11:
Apostolic Culture

SECTION 12:
Summary & Conclusion

www.KingdomHouse.net

KINGDOM HOUSE
P U B L I S H I N G

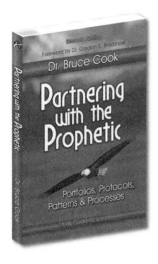

ALSO BY DR. BRUCE COOK

Finally, the one book on the prophetic that I can use both in my graduate level course on 5-Fold Ministry at Regent University, as well as in the equipping ministries in the churches that I oversee. In a time of traveling light, this is the one book on the prophetic that will give you focus and passion for its full restoration.

Dr. Joseph Umidi |
Professor, Overseer, CEO

Partnering with the Prophetic is a resource that every student or minister of the prophetic should have in their library. Bruce skillfully teaches, instructs, and imparts faith for activation in this timely book. I have witnessed the operation of Bruce Cook's prophetic gift and received prophetic blessing and encouragement from God through him. Both Bruce and his gift are authentic—true gifts to the Body of Christ.

Patricia King | Co-Founder of XPmedia

Prophets are not the only ones who need to understand the prophetic. The whole body needs to understand the prophetic and allow the Holy Spirit to move in that way. *Partnering with the Prophetic* will bring clarity and unity to the church. It will give us ... a release, a great understanding to our native people that believe in the prophetic, which they call THE DREAMER.

Dr. Negiel Bigpond | *Morning Star Church of All Nations*
Co-founder Two Rivers Native American Training Center

www.KingdomHouse.net

KINGDOM HOUSE
PUBLISHING

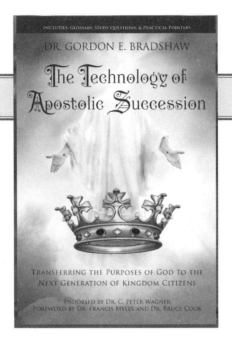

THE TECHNOLOGY OF APOSTOLIC SUCCESSION
TRANSFERRING THE PURPOSES OF GOD TO THE
NEXT GENERATION OF KINGDOM CITIZENS
DR. GORDON BRADSHAW

"God is assembling something in our day that is so silent and massive that it can only be discerned by those who have felt the shaping of God's chisel in the quarry. Gordon Bradshaw has given us a work that reflects years of shaping and consecrated thought, measuring and carefully layering line upon line until a great architectural blueprint is drawn."

Dr. Lance Wallnau

Founder & President, The Lance Learning Group

www.KingdomHouse.net

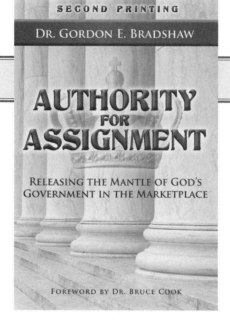

AUTHORITY FOR ASSIGNMENT
RELEASING THE MANTLE OF GOD'S
GOVERNMENT IN THE MARKETPLACE
DR. GORDON BRADSHAW

How will "God's Government" affect the marketplace today?

It will come through the restoration of one of God's greatest supernatural technologies ... "The Mantle of Misrah!" Misrah is a Hebrew word that means "government and prevailing power." Inside this powerful mantle we've been given a supernatural problem-solving dynamic that restores the marketplace to its highest level of function for the Kingdom of God!

www.KingdomHouse.net